THE
250
PERSONAL
FINANCE
QUESTIONS
FOR YOUR
20s & 30s

DEBBY FOWLES

Aadamsmedia

Avon, Massachusetts

Published by Adams Media, an F+W Media Company
57 Littlefield Street, Avon, MA 02322. U.S.A.
www.adamsmedia.com

Contains material adapted and abridged from *The Everything® Personal Finance in Your 20s and 30s Book* by Debby Fowles, copyright © 2003 by F+W Publications, Inc., and *The Everything® Personal Finance in Your 20s and 30s Book, 2nd Edition* by Debby Fowles, copyright © 2008 by F+W Publications, Inc.

ISBN 10: 1-59869-863-X
ISBN 13: 978-1-59869-863-3

Printed in Canada.

J I H G F E D C B A

Library of Congress Cataloging-in-Publication Data
is available from the publisher.

This publication is designed to provide accurate and authoritative information with regard to the subject matter covered. It is sold with the understanding that the publisher is not engaged in rendering legal, accounting, or other professional advice. If legal advice or other expert assistance is required, the services of a competent professional person should be sought.
   —From a *Declaration of Principles* jointly adopted by a Committee of the American Bar Association and a Committee of Publishers and Associations

Many of the designations used by manufacturers and sellers to distinguish their products are claimed as trademarks. Where those designations appear in this book and Adams Media was aware of a trademark claim, the designations have been printed with initial capital letters.

This book is available at quantity discounts for bulk purchases.
For information, call 1-800-289-0963.

CONTENTS

PART IV: PLANNING FOR TOMORROW

INTRODUCTION

How do you learn how to save money and make it grow? How do you evaluate offers and deals and make wise choices? If you practice the basic personal-finance guidelines and concepts outlined in this book, you can become financially savvy and financially secure. You can learn to avoid the financial mistakes that can have such a negative impact on your future and your relationships. The book will show you how to live more simply, save more money, spend less, avoid impulse spending and credit card debt, stick to a realistic spending plan (budget), and plan for your retirement—without making huge sacrifices while you're doing it.

Your twenties are the best time to develop good personal-finance habits, before you get into debt that you'd have to struggle to pay off or make other financial mistakes that you'd spend years recovering from. In your thirties, it's still not too late to turn your financial life around if you're not on the right track.

There is little that's more rewarding than seeing your financial goals and dreams becoming a reality. Controlling your money instead of letting your money control you gives you a sense of empowerment and self-esteem. Watching your investments grow and knowing you have a nest egg to fall back on gives you a sense of security. In the end, you don't really give up anything of lasting importance. You gain everything that really matters to you.

If you're not too deeply in debt yet, your rapid progress will be its own reward. If you are deeply in debt, you'll have to work at it harder and longer, but it can be work that's empowering, stress relieving, and even fun. It all comes down to balance and making smart decisions about money. It gets easier with practice and is hugely rewarding, both financially and emotionally. Why not get started now?

Getting Started

Chapter 1

SETTING GOALS

You wouldn't start out on a long trip into unfamiliar territory without a road map, yet many people go through life without a concrete plan for their financial future. The road to financial freedom can lead directly to your destination or to a dead end. Specific financial goals and written plans for meeting them help you focus your efforts on the end result.

Goals are like the wheels on your car; they keep you moving in the direction you want to go, and you won't get very far without them. If you haven't already started planning for your future, now's the time to begin, no matter what your age. If you're in your twenties, however, you have a distinct advantage. Saving and investing in your twenties will give you the most powerful financial tool available: time. You'll have to work at it a lot harder if you start later in life. In fact, the smartest thing you can do in your twenties is save and invest. Ultimately, you'll have to save and invest a lot less money at a time and will still come out far ahead of the person who starts a decade or two later.

Question 1: **Why do I need to set financial goals?**

All successful organizations have short- and long-term goals and a written plan for reaching them, and if you want to be financially successful, so should you. The first steps are to determine your financial status today and then decide what you want to achieve for your future and how you're going to accomplish it. Starting in your twenties is a huge advantage. If you invest $5,000 at the age of twenty, and it earns 7 percent per year, at retirement (age sixty-five) it will total over $115,000. The same amount invested at the age of forty would total less than $29,000. As the saying goes, "Most people don't plan to fail, they just fail to plan." Without planning, even the best of intentions lead nowhere. Start mapping out your route now. Your entire future depends on it.

Question 2: **What should I do first?**

As with any road map, before you can determine how to get from here to there, you need to know where "here" is. Where do you stand financially? Answering this critical question is the job of the net worth statement. The net worth statement is very simple in concept. Your net worth is the difference between all the things of value that you own and all the debts you owe, or in financial terms, your assets minus your liabilities. Your net worth statement is a list of each of these items and their current value or balance.

Question 3: **Why do I need a net worth statement?**

The net worth statement gives you a snapshot of your financial condition at this moment in time. You need this information in order to effectively set the financial goals that you'll be working toward, assess your progress along the way, and make adjustments, using the important clues gleaned from updating your net worth statement on a regular basis. It will also come in handy when applying for a mortgage, credit card, or car loan.

Sometimes people avoid making a list of their debts because they're afraid they won't like what they find or they believe they already have a good "gut feel" for their overall financial picture. However, burying your head in the sand like the proverbial ostrich won't get you far, and gut feelings can be way off the mark. Not having a handle on your financial condition can seriously hurt you in a time of crisis, like a job loss or disability, and it's difficult if not impossible to plan for the future if you don't know where you are today.

Question 4: **How do I create my net worth statement?**

Start by listing all the things of value that you own, even if you owe money on them, like your house and cars. Use their full value as of today. The balances of the loans related to these assets will be included in the liabilities section, so your equity in the assets you list won't be overstated. For bonds, stock options, and retirement accounts, use the current value, not the value at maturity or the value on the date you're fully vested.

You should receive statements showing the current value of your accounts from your employer for retirement accounts and from your broker for bonds. The human resources department where you work can help you determine the current value of your company stock options if you're lucky enough to have them.

Question 5: **Should I include my life insurance policy in my net worth statement?**

List only those life insurance policies that have a cash value. Most life insurance policies are provided by employers and are term policies good only for the time you're employed by that company. These are not considered assets. If you've purchased cash-value life insurance from an agent and you're unsure of the current cash value, he or she should be able to help you determine the amount you would get if you cashed it in today. Use that amount for your net worth statement.

Question 6: **Where can I find out what my car is worth?**

For cars and other vehicles, use the *Kelley Blue Book* value, which is the estimated price the car would sell for if sold privately to another consumer or to a car dealer. You can look up *Kelley Blue Book* values at the library or online at *www.kbb.com*. For all other assets, use your best estimate of the fair market value, which is the price a willing, rational, and knowledgeable buyer would pay. Fair market value may be more or less than you paid for the item and is the most meaningful measure of its current worth.

Question 7: **What do I do after I list all my assets?**

Now you've listed everything you own that has a monetary value, but the total is not a true representation of your financial worth. It doesn't take into account the money you may owe banks or finance companies before you really own some of your assets—like your house or car, for example. It also doesn't yet take into account the money that you owe to other creditors. These are called your liabilities. Keep reading to further understand the process of figuring in your liabilities.

Question 8: **Now that I've listed my assets and liabilities, how do I calculate my net worth?**

When you've listed everything you can think of, total the assets, then total the liabilities. Now, subtract your liabilities from your assets. If the number is positive (assets are greater than liabilities), you have a positive net worth. Congratulations! Now you can start working on building that net worth. If the number is negative (liabilities are greater than assets), you have a negative net worth, but don't let it discourage you. Now that you know exactly where you stand, you can map out your route to a positive net worth.

Question 9: **If I have a negative net worth, should I use my savings to pay off some of my debts?**

Most of us struggle with the question of whether to use available funds to pay off long-term debt, such as paying down the balance on a mortgage, or to use them for short-term goals, such as building an emergency fund. The answer is to find a balance between the two. This takes thoughtful consideration of your short- and long-term goals, careful planning, and making adjustments in your plans as your goals and your financial situation change.

Question 10: **What should my financial goals be?**

Think seriously about what you want to achieve. Do you envision retiring while you're still young enough to enjoy travel or an active lifestyle? Would you like to buy your first home or move up to a larger home in a better neighborhood? Is having a vacation home in the mountains or on the beach your dream? In the shorter term, maybe a new car or a boat is on your wish list. What's important to you?

Your goals should be just that: *your* goals, not your parents' or your friends'. Don't choose goals just because they sound like what you should want. The question is, do you really want them? Do you want them badly enough to give up the instant gratification of spending all your money now for the future enjoyment of having what is really meaningful to you later?

Your financial goals may include saving for a down payment on a house, making home improvements, buying a new vehicle, paying off a loan, saving for graduate school or for your kids' college education, putting away some money for a dream vacation, or saving for a large purchase. You may have the goal of being able to afford for you or your spouse to stay home with your kids. In short, your goals should reflect your own values and dreams.

Question 11: **I have a long list of goals—which ones should I start working toward first?**

You may have a list of long-term goals (goals you expect to meet in five years or more). You can break these goals down into short-term goals (one year or less), making it easier to stay focused on the future and giving you a sense of accomplishment and satisfaction along the way. In some cases, you may also want to identify a medium-term goal (one to three years).

Don't let fear of failure cause you to set goals that aren't ambitious enough. You want to stretch yourself a little to reach your goal, but you have to believe that it's possible or you won't stay motivated for long. Try to strike a balance.

Whatever your goal, simply dreaming about it won't make it happen. A goal should be written down and reviewed often. Written goals give you something to work toward and make your efforts to save more meaningful, but figuring out how to achieve your goals is just as important as stating them.

Include a description of the goal, the time frame for achieving it, the amount of money needed, the amount already saved, and your plan for achieving the goal (for example, putting aside $100 a month, working ten hours of overtime a week, cutting entertainment costs in half, or getting a second job). Having a deadline for achieving your goal creates a sense of urgency that makes it easier to stay focused.

Question 12: **How will I know if I'm making any progress?**

You've prepared a net worth statement, thought about what you want to achieve in life, identified some goals, and broken them down into short- and long-term goals. You're well on your way. Now you need to determine how you'll evaluate your progress. You'll probably have a sense of whether you're making progress on your goals from month to month, but take the time to sit down at least monthly after you've updated your budget for the month and review how you're doing. Long-term goals can be reviewed less frequently than short-term goals because your timeframe for achieving them is longer, but more frequent reviews allow you to spot problems earlier and take corrective action if you're falling short of where you want to be.

It's easy to get off track or drift along without making any real progress if all you have is a few vague dreams, so when writing down your goals, do it in enough detail to give yourself a visual each time you read it. If you're saving to buy a house, don't just write down "buy our own house." Write so you can almost see it: "I want to buy a cozy cape with a water view on two or more wooded acres on the coast of Maine." Each time you think of this goal, picture this cozy cape in your mind in as much detail as possible. The more you can imagine what meeting your goal will look like, feel like, and smell like, the better chance you have of achieving it.

Question 13: **What should I do if I fall behind on achieving my goals?**

If you find yourself falling short of your goals because you just don't feel motivated enough to stick with your plan, try making a list of all the benefits of succeeding in your goal, and review them often. Don't underestimate the power of your subconscious to help you stay motivated. Put positive thoughts in your mind about your goals and they'll be easier to attain.

Remember to make the goals specific. Ask yourself how you'll know when you've reached each of your goals. If you can come up with a concrete, measurable answer, you're on the right track.

After you've written down as many goals as you can think of, choose two or three short-term and two or three long-term goals to work on this year. Let's say you choose building a retirement fund as one of your most important long-term goals. To break it down into short-term goals, set a monthly goal to contribute a set dollar amount to your employer's 401(k) or other retirement plan.

Question 14: **Where can I find good information on personal finance?**

Books like this are one source. Check your local bookstore or an online bookstore like Amazon.com, searching for keywords like "personal finance" or "money management." Magazines are another source. The bookstands are filled with financial magazines. Some of them are definitely for people who are avid investors or interested in business financial news, but thumb through a few and see if any of them seem readable and interesting. If you find one, consider subscribing to it.

Question 15: **Can I find trustworthy information on the Internet?**

The Internet is a source of nearly limitless information, some of it excellent. Try to stick with well-known sites rather than the folksy "this is how I did it" personal sites. Although the latter can have useful information on them, you could be steered in the wrong direction with some questionable advice or information. On the other hand, the personal sites about frugal living, downsizing, and cutting costs can be great for giving you ideas on how to do the same.

The less financially savvy you are, the more vulnerable you are to being taken advantage of or falling victim to financial scams. Not everything you read is true, so it's important to use reputable sources of information and practice some healthy skepticism if something sounds too good to be true.

Chapter 2

BUILDING A BUDGET

BUDGET. FOR SOME, the word conjures up images of sacrifice, penny-pinching, and doing without. The most important ingredient in a successful budget is a positive attitude. At least 50 percent of budgeting is mental, so if the word makes you shudder, work on replacing this negative image with a positive one. If you've failed at budgeting in the past, ask yourself whether your budget was simply a review of how you spent your money after it was already gone, rather than a plan for spending and saving. The former is ineffective and frustrating. The latter is freeing and rewarding.

Part of meeting your goals is being able to create a budget and stick to it. Budgeting consists of setting up spending categories, tracking your expenditures, monitoring your progress, making adjustments, plugging spending leaks, and staying motivated. Your chances of being financially successful without budgeting are slim. It takes time and effort, but the rewards are tremendous.

Question 16: **Why do I need to create a budget?**

A budget is really a spending plan. You may struggle with an unrealistic plan to save thousands of dollars when what you really need to do is spend more wisely. If you think you can meet your financial goals without a spending plan, you will most likely be disappointed. Creating a spending plan is the first and most basic step you can take toward putting your money to work for you, regardless of whether you make thousands of dollars or hundreds of thousands of dollars a year.

Attitude matters. Think of budgeting as eating right rather than being on a diet. You eat what you want in moderate amounts, you don't binge, you don't deprive yourself, and yet you end up better off.

Question 17: **What are the benefits of budgeting?**

Budgeting and tracking your expenses shows you where your money goes and how seemingly inconsequential daily or weekly expenditures can add up over time. By tracking all of your expenditures, you can make conscious decisions about how to spend or invest your money instead of dribbling it away a dollar or two at a time. This can be the difference between never having enough money and being able to afford the things that are really important to you, like saving for a down payment on a house, buying a new car, paying off credit card debt, planning for retirement, or saving for that trip to Cancun.

Having a working budget can greatly reduce the stress in your life that revolves around money issues. You'll know what you can or can't afford. You'll feel confident that you'll be able to pay your bills when they're due, or you'll have advance warning that there's going to be a problem, giving you time to plan alternatives.

An unexpected side benefit of budgeting is that it can improve your relationship with your spouse or partner. Money matters are the single largest cause of marital discord and divorce, so getting a grip on spending by coming to an agreement about your financial goals and working together toward those goals can have a positive effect on your relationship.

Question 18: **What goes into making a good budget?**

A good spending plan is flexible and realistic. It's a road map that offers alternative routes to your destination, depending on your personal road conditions. It should be dynamic, changing to fit your needs. If you have no kids, you wouldn't use the same budget as someone who does; if you live in rented housing, you wouldn't use the same budget as someone who owns their home. Life changes, and so should your budget.

The complexity level of a good budgeting system should match the level of your time and interest. Some people love recording the details. If you're not one of them, choose a simpler approach so it's not too much of a chore. The objective is to come up with a system you can live with for a long time.

Question 19: **What should I include in my budget?**

It's a good idea to put together a budget worksheet to get started in setting up your budget. You'll get some help on doing it here, but make sure the categories you use fit your personal lifestyle. Use the basic common categories that apply to everyone, such as housing, utilities, insurance, and food, but customize the other categories to fit your personal situation.

Your categories should be detailed enough to provide you with useful information, but not so detailed that you become bogged down in trivia. First, list all your sources of income:

- Wages from your job(s)
- Bonuses
- Child support or alimony
- Rental income
- Interest income
- Dividend income
- Capital gains income
- Other income

Next, list the expense categories you want to track. Start out with a little more detail rather than a little less. You can always combine categories later if you find expenditures in one category are so small that they don't warrant being tracked separately.

Question 20: **How can I save money when my budget shows me that I spend all my income?**

The first rule of personal finance is to pay yourself first. Make savings an expense category, with a set amount that you pay to yourself monthly when you pay your bills. Don't plan your savings around what's left over when you've paid everything else. Chances are, there won't be anything there.

To curtail overspending, you need to set realistic spending goals in each category. First, figure out how much money you have available, and where that money goes now. To get started, collect as many of your pay stubs, bills, credit card statements, and receipts as possible for the last three months and complete the income section of your budget.

Question 21: **How do I figure out where all my money is going?**

In addition to bills, credit card statements, and receipts, your checkbook register will be important in completing the expense portion of the worksheet. Go through these documents and jot down your expenditures in each of the categories you've set up, then total the numbers in each category and transfer them to the worksheet. For the items you identified that aren't paid every month, calculate the yearly cost and divide it by twelve to get the monthly cost for your budget worksheet. Each month, set aside the monthly amount in a savings account so it's available when the bill becomes due.

To really get a fix on where your money goes, you'll need to keep track of your cash expenditures, too. Save receipts to record later, or jot the expenditure down on a notepad as you use cash. The more often you use an ATM, the more important it is to write down your cash expenditures, because this is where many people lose control of where their money goes. Tracking your cash expenditures is one of the more tedious aspects of budgeting, but it's where you have the most potential for budget leaks, and most people are surprised if not shocked when they see how much cash slips through their hands each month.

Question 22: **Do I have to keep track of all the little things, like my daily cup of coffee?**

You may think you know where your money goes, but most people are more than a little surprised when they really start tracking their expenses. Small cash expenditures can add up to significant sums of money by month's end. That daily cup of coffee is probably costing you almost $400 per year. Three six-packs of beer a week adds up to at least $600. If you smoke two packs of cigarettes a day, it's probably costing you over $280 a month, $3,360 per year, or $33,600 in ten years—and that's if you discount the impact of inflation!

If you invested $280 every month instead of spending it on cigarettes, beer, or other common habits, and it earned a modest 5 percent return starting when you were thirty years old, by the time you reached retirement age you would have over $319,000! Think of what you could do with that money.

Question 23: **How can I use my budget to save money?**

After a month or two of tracking your actual spending, you'll begin to see a pattern, and you can identify where you can comfortably make adjustments to start saving money. Consider this a process of self-discovery. You can start with an in-depth look at your largest spending categories if you prefer, but don't overlook the smaller categories. Sometimes these are the easiest to make cuts in because the spending may be more discretionary, and small amounts can add up quickly.

Identify areas where you can painlessly save money that you can use to build an emergency fund or save for an important goal. Brainstorm about ways to reduce spending in specific categories. Cutting costs becomes a challenge that can be very rewarding, especially as you see your savings grow.

Question 24: **How much should I be spending in each category?**

Once you feel comfortable that you know where your money is going and you've identified some ways to cut costs in a number of categories, establish a monthly spending target for each category. Do your fixed expenses first, like your mortgage and car payment. Then look at each of your remaining budget categories and set a spending target, taking into consideration what you know about your own spending habits and where you can cut back without causing a hardship.

An important part of budgeting is coming up with concrete ways to cut costs. Setting a spending limit with no thought about how to reduce expenses will be an exercise in frustration as you review your failures monthly. Come up with innovative ways to put money in your own pocket.

Question 25: **How do I know if I'll have enough money at the end of the month?**

When you've set a tentative target for each category, subtotal the income and expense categories and subtract the total expenses from the total income to arrive at your net income. This will be the amount of money you have left over for building an emergency fund, making additional payments on your credit cards, and working on your other financial goals, assuming you've recorded all of your income and expenditures accurately. If the number is negative, your expenses are greater than your income. Don't be discouraged. Your situation can no doubt be greatly improved by tweaking your spending habits. If you have a positive net income, be sure to transfer most of it to a savings or investment account at the end of each month. Extra cash left in a regular checking account has a way of getting spent.

Question 26: **What should I do if I can't stick to a monthly budget?**

If you find you've exceeded your budget for the month, don't despair. Use it as a learning experience to improve your budgeting for the future. Your budget will get more refined every month and you'll get better and better at managing your money and working toward your goals. If you find after a month or two that tracking your expenses is too much work, consider combining some categories, such as miscellaneous household expenses or utilities, to reduce the record keeping, rather than giving up.

As you readjust the categories, look for areas where you can save small amounts of money. Small savings are easier to find and easier to implement than large ones, and small victories will give you a positive feeling about budgeting before you get into the tough stuff. Remember, the idea is not to deprive yourself, but to funnel as much of your money as possible toward the goals that are most important to you. As your personal situation changes, reflect those changes in your budget.

Question 27: **How can I cut back on essentials, like groceries?**

Grocery shopping is one area ripe for cost cutting. Do you buy a lot of prepared foods instead of doing the cooking yourself? There's a tradeoff between the cost and the convenience of prepared foods when you're too busy to cook. Snacks are another expensive item, especially if you buy the serving-size packages to include in the kids' school lunches. Consider buying bulk and using baggies. Buy generic brands. Use coupons.

Do the workers at the fast-food restaurants in town know you by name? If eating out is a lifestyle instead of a treat, consider cutting back on fast food and enjoying a monthly dinner out with your spouse or a friend. You'll feel like you've treated yourself, and you'll probably end up spending less money than if you regularly buy fast food.

What's the deductible on your auto insurance? It should be at least $250, and if you have a good driving record, $500 is even better. The certain cost of paying higher insurance for a lower deductible weighed against the likelihood of having an accident may not be to your advantage. If the car is more than eight years old, consider dropping collision coverage altogether, and just keep liability coverage on that vehicle. The cost of collision coverage on a car that is worth only a few thousand dollars is out of proportion to the benefit you receive, especially if you have a good driving record.

Question 28: **Do I need to use a software program to manage my money?**

If you're willing to invest the time, a personal-finance software program can bring your money management to a whole new level, but you don't need to do more than the basics if you don't have the time or interest. Unless you have very few expenses and they're relatively simple, a good software program will make the job of tracking everything easier and less time-consuming. Being able to print out graphs and reports from your PC with the click of a button can serve as a motivation for entering all that data. If you don't want to use a computer, that's okay too. It's entirely possible to budget successfully with paper and pencil.

Some of the most popular personal-finance software programs for automating your checkbook and tracking your expenses are Quicken, Microsoft Money, and Moneydance. These are available online or at big office supply stores like Staples.

Microsoft Money and Quicken are both user-friendly programs with many features you'll probably never use, but they're also great programs for the average person who just wants to do online banking, automatically reconcile their bank statement, track expenses, budget, prepare for tax time, and print reports. The budget versus the actual report alone is worth the investment. Moneydance is a simpler program that is not as well known, but it provides the same basic features without all the fancy bells and whistles.

Question 29: **What can I do to stay motivated and keep to my budget?**

Your budget won't work unless you stick with it. One of the keys to staying motivated is keeping the budgeting process from being too complex or time consuming (unless you or another family member enjoys tracking the details). Make budgeting a family activity and involve each family member in some way. Reward yourself for reaching saving and spending goals and making progress on paying down debt.

One of the most rewarding things about budgeting is seeing results every month. This is easy if you use personal-finance software, because once you enter your expenditures and income for the month, a click of the mouse produces reports that show budgeted versus actual expenses by category, your new and improved net worth, balances in savings and investment accounts, and more. You can even print or view colorful graphs and pie charts for a visual look at how you're doing.

Don't forget to work on your attitude each month as well as your spending plan. Give yourself a pat on the back for the increases in your savings and other assets and the decreases in your credit card debt and loan balances. Remind yourself of the importance of your real goals. The budget is just a tool that increases your awareness of where your money goes and provides guidelines for spending so your money goes toward the things that are most meaningful to you.

Chapter 3

SAVING MONEY

WITHOUT A SAVINGS plan, the chances of saving enough money to meet long-term financial goals are very slim. Like financial success, saving money doesn't happen by accident. It requires smart buying, cutting costs, planning, and understanding a few basic financial concepts like the magic of compounding, the Rule of 72, the time value of money, and the danger of inflation. It can also be fun and interesting to keep track of the money you save by practicing frugality. Try keeping tabs on how much you save each time you make informed buying decisions or abstain from buying an item you would have bought before you came up with your spending plan.

Question 30: **Why should I worry about saving money now?**

The magic of compounding is the biggest reason it's so important to start saving in your early twenties. People who wait until their forties to start saving will have to save much more than those who started in their twenties. What's worse, they will never be able to catch up with those who started in their twenties without saving and investing drastically higher amounts than would have been necessary had they started at a younger age.

Question 31: **What is compound interest?**

There are two basic methods of calculating interest: simple interest and compound interest. Simple interest is calculated based only on your initial investment. Compounding means that as you earn interest on your investment, it is added to your original investment, and as a result you earn interest on your interest as well. The difference may not seem like much, but the effect that compounding can have over a long period of time is astounding, especially with larger initial investments and higher rates of return.

To illustrate how compounding works, assume you invest $1,000 at 10 percent interest compounded annually. At the end of the first year, you'll have earned $100, for a total of $1,100. At the end of year two, the interest is calculated on $1,100, so you'll earn $110, for a balance of $1,210.

Question 32: **How is compound interest calculated?**

Interest is usually compounded annually, monthly, or daily. The more frequently compounding takes place, the faster your money will grow. As the balance grows larger, the difference between simple interest and compound interest becomes greater. Let's say you put $5,000 in an account that earns 10 percent interest. Here's what your investment would be worth at the end of ten years if you didn't add another penny to it:

* Compounded annually: $12,968
* Compounded monthly: $13,535
* Compounded daily: $13,589

To illustrate the effect of a longer period of time on compounding, consider Bill, who contributed $2,000 at 6 percent interest to an IRA beginning at the age of twenty-two and continued doing so each year until he was thirty (nine years). By the time he was sixty-five, his $18,000 investment had grown to over $579,000. His friend Jim made a $2,000 contribution every year for thirty-five years, for a total of $70,000, but because he started at the age of thirty-one, his nest egg only totaled $470,000. Even though he contributed much more than Bill ($70,000 versus Bill's $18,000) he ended up with 23 percent less money.

Question 33: **What is the Rule of 72?**

The Rule of 72 is a nifty mathematical computation used to estimate how long it will take a certain sum of money to double at a certain interest rate (assuming the interest is compounded annually). You can use this simple rule to quickly determine how long it will take your savings or an investment to double, or how long it will take a debt to double. Try it out on some of your investments or debts.

Question 34: **How does the Rule of 72 work?**

To calculate how quickly your investment will double, divide 72 by the interest rate or expected rate of return. The result is the number of years it will take your money to double at that interest rate, assuming you reinvest your earnings. So if your money is invested at 8 percent interest, you make the following quick calculation: 72 ÷ 8 = 9. This means it will take approximately nine years.

Question 35: **In what other ways can I use the Rule of 72?**

You can use the Rule of 72 to see how long it will take your credit card or other debt to double, too. If you have a $5,000 credit card balance with an interest rate of 10 percent, your debt will double in 7.2 years. If the interest rate is 19 percent, your debt will double in 3.8 years. If you're only paying the minimum payment each month, it doesn't take long for your balance to double.

You can also use the Rule of 72 to estimate what rate of return you'd need to earn in order for your money to double in a certain number of years; for example, ten years: 72 ÷ 10 = 7.2, so you'd need to earn 7.2 percent annually for your money to double in ten years.

Question 36: **What is inflation?**

Inflation is the effect of rising prices on your buying power. Inflation is often left out of the equation when calculating how much money you'll have available at some point down the road, but it can have a serious negative impact on the buying power of your money. The average inflation rate since 1994 has been approximately 2.5 percent, but in the early 1980s, we experienced double-digit inflation. Since 1980, the price of goods and services has increased 80 percent, so an item that cost $100 in 1980 costs $180 in 2002. Since much of our financial planning is done for years into the future, it's important to consider the impact of inflation when determining how much money you'll need in retirement, for example.

Question 37: **How does inflation affect me?**

You can use the Rule of 72 to estimate the real buying power of a sum of money at some point in the future, taking inflation into consideration. If the inflation rate is 4 percent, prices will double in eighteen years (72 ÷ 4 = 18), so if you plan to retire in eighteen years and you need $3,000 a month in today's money, you'd need $6,000 a month to retain the same buying power you have today.

The $30,000 salary you earn this year will be worth only $28,800 next year if inflation is 4 percent. If you're fortunate, you'll get a salary increase annually that at least keeps pace with the rate of inflation; otherwise you fall further behind each year.

Question 38: **What does "the time value of money" mean?**

The time value of money is a basic financial concept based on the assumption that a dollar received today is worth more than a dollar received at some future date because a dollar received today can be invested and earn interest. If someone agreed to pay you $1,000 ten years from now, or some lesser amount today, you could calculate the amount you'd need to receive today to equal the value of $1,000 in ten years.

There's more to the concept of the time value of money, but the most important thing for you to remember is that receiving $1 today is better than receiving $1 tomorrow, and the entire amount in a lump sum is better than installment payments (assuming there's no interest involved). If you're paid in installments, you lose the opportunity to invest the lump sum for a longer period of time.

Question 39: **Do I really need an emergency fund?**

More than ever, in these uncertain times, everyone should have an emergency fund. Financial advisors suggest having enough savings in an easily accessible account to cover your living expenses for three to six months. Having this financial safety net will give you peace of mind about how you'll meet your most basic financial obligations in the event of illness, job loss, or other serious emergency. The fund can also be used for unplanned expenses such as major house or car repairs, or medical costs not covered by insurance. In a volatile job market, an emergency fund is more critical than ever.

Now that you have a budget in place, you can easily calculate how much money you'd need to cover your basic, no-frills living expenses if you had a sudden loss of income. Write down your goal for your emergency fund and decide on an amount to contribute to it each month, using the "pay yourself first" rule. If possible, keep the fund in a separate account, such as a money market account, so you're less tempted to dip into it. Since emergency funds might be needed without notice, they should be kept in liquid accounts that are easy to cash in quickly.

Question 40: **I can barely cover my living expenses each month—how can I save anything?**

Don't be discouraged if you currently have no extra money to put away. The secret to saving money is that there's no secret involved at all. By developing a realistic budget, setting spending and savings goals, and sticking to them, you can create money for savings. Decide on a percentage of your income to designate as savings. Financial planners suggest 10 percent, but if 8 or 5 percent is all you can handle at this time, start with that.

Question 41: **If I can only save a few dollars each month, should I even bother?**

Don't make the mistake of thinking that if you can't save a large amount of money all at once, it's not worthwhile to try. This couldn't be further from the truth. If you saved $25 a month at 6 percent interest, in five years you'd have $1,744. If you saved $100 a month at 6 percent interest, in five years you'd have $6,977; in ten years, you'd have $16,388. Even if you think you can't possibly save this much each month, you'll be surprised how much more money is available for savings as you continue to refine your budgeting and spending plans. It's okay to stretch to the point of discomfort, but saving shouldn't be painful to the point of making you do without things you truly need.

Question 42: **What should I do to start saving?**

Set up a separate savings account. If you mingle your day-to-day funds with your savings, it's almost inevitable that you'll end up using some or all of the savings, and you may never repay them. There's also a mental component. Seeing your savings balance grow from month to month and your financial goals becoming more of a reality is highly motivating.

If you have direct deposit at work and your employer allows you to split your deposit, consider having a set amount deducted from your paycheck and deposited in a savings account. It's much easier to save when the money doesn't have to take a detour to your checking account before reaching your savings account. If you don't have this option, write yourself a check every month before you pay your bills, and deposit it to your savings account.

Use windfalls to pump up your savings instead of spending them. Bonuses, tax refunds, rebates, overtime pay, income from hobbies or yard sales, cash gifts from family, lottery winnings, and other sporadic cash receipts can make faster advances toward your goals without requiring additional spending cutbacks. When you receive a salary increase, put all or part of it into savings each pay period and continue living on your previous salary. When you pay off a loan, continue putting the payment amount aside each month, but pay it into your savings account instead of to the bank or finance company. Because you're already in the habit of doing without that money, you won't even miss it.

Question 43: **What if there is no room in my budget for saving?**

You may think there's no fat in your budget, but nearly everyone can find some if they look hard enough. Consider it a challenge to find ways to cut your expenses, or make a game of it. If you smoke, why not quit? Smoking is one of the most expensive habits you can have; many couples spend as much on cigarettes as they would on a new car payment each month.

Speaking of car payments, ask yourself if you really need the gas-guzzling SUV you drive. You could save considerable money on gas, repairs, and maintenance, as well as insurance, not to mention your monthly car payment, if you bought a less expensive, more fuel-efficient vehicle.

Consider buying things used instead of new. Check the classifieds for things like exercise equipment, vehicles, musical instruments, electronics, and more. There are always people who have made the mistake you're trying to avoid by buying something they ended up not wanting or needing. You can often get great bargains on items that may be as good as new.

The list of ways to save money is endless. As you get into the habit of questioning every expense and looking for ways to cut costs, you'll develop a saving mindset and you'll see the savings add up. You've discovered the "secret" to saving.

Chapter 4

BANKING WITH CONFIDENCE

You PROBABLY HAVE a checking account and maybe a savings account, but chances are you don't give much thought to the impact banking has on your finances. Being knowledgeable about how banks work can save you money. You might be surprised just how much your banking arrangements and habits are costing you. When it comes to choosing a bank, consider both convenience and cost. Find out what types of fees the bank charges. Some charge flat monthly fees; others charge a fee for each check written and each deposit made. Some charge if you go below the minimum balance, use a live teller, use another bank's automated teller machine (ATM), make an account balance inquiry, have your canceled checks returned to you each month, or close your account. Most charge for bouncing checks, placing a stop payment on a check, and using your overdraft protection.

Question 44: **How do I choose the right bank for me?**

Review your banking habits, identify the services that are most important to you, compare fees for those services between several different banks, and then choose the bank that fits your needs for the best price. If you use ATMs to withdraw cash from your account on a weekly basis, for example, you wouldn't want to choose a bank that offers free checking but charges a hefty fee for ATM transactions. You may decide to use a traditional brick-and-mortar bank in your neighborhood or an Internet bank in cyberspace.

Online banking allows you to view all your banking transactions, making it easy to update your checkbook register and ensure that you didn't forget to record any ATM withdrawals, deposits, or other transactions. Many people use this feature instead of actually reconciling their bank statement the old-fashioned way. If you're interested in trying online banking, contact your bank for information on how to begin.

There are two ways to bank online. Internet-based banking systems allow you to dial in to the bank's computer using any computer with a modem and use the bank's software to look at your account balance and transactions. Client-based systems require you to download information from the bank into personal-finance software that resides on your computer's hard drive. Internet banking is the way of the future, so if you're thinking of changing banks, you might save yourself time and trouble by choosing one with Internet-based banking.

Question 45: **Should I consider using a credit union?**

In today's world, you've got a few options when it comes to banking. One such option is to pick a credit union over a traditional bank. Banks are owned by investors; credit unions are owned and controlled by customers, who are members. Credit unions are nonprofit organizations and return surplus earnings to members by lowering interest rates on loans, increasing interest rates on deposits, or offering free or low-cost services.

Question 46: **How do I know my money will be safe?**

The most basic requirement for any bank or credit union you choose is that it must be a member of the Federal Deposit Insurance Corporation (FDIC), which is fully backed by the U.S. government. This ensures that your account will be protected for up to $100,000. Go to the FDIC website at *www.fdic.gov*, click on "Is My Bank Insured?" and enter the official name, city, and state of the bank, then click the "Find My Institution" button.

Reconcile your checkbook monthly and review your credit card statements for errors. Scam artists are finding new ways to target these two areas and if you're not alert, you could get taken for a ride.

Even if you don't bank online, you may use automatic debits to have payment for one or more of your bills automatically deducted from your checking account each month. To protect yourself from automatic debit scams, never give out your bank account number or other information printed on your check to anyone over the telephone. If you do, they may use it to fraudulently remove money from your account. If you believe you've been the victim of an automatic debit scam, contact your bank immediately.

Question 47: **What are opportunity costs?**

Opportunity costs are the benefits you lose by not choosing the best alternative for the use of your money. If you pay $100 in credit card interest each month, you've lost not just $100, but also the added value you could have received if you had invested that $100.

When your money could be earning more somewhere else, that's called opportunity costs. You may not be paying any fees directly, but you've lost an opportunity to make money elsewhere. For example, the balance that you maintain in your checking account to avoid a monthly fee could be earning more than the monthly fee if invested in a money market account or certificate of deposit (CD).

Question 48: **How can I reduce the costs of banking?**

Sometimes you can gain as much by cutting seemingly insignificant costs that add up over time as you can by earning additional income. Banking costs are a good example. Banks charge so many different types of fees, some of them hidden, that you may not realize what your real costs are.

With minimum balance requirements, ATM fees, overdraft charges, and other fees, even your basic checking and savings accounts might be costing you more than they should.

Learn about the different banking features and then pay only for the ones that truly make sense for you. Be aware of your banking costs and make intelligent tradeoffs to get the services you use for the lowest overall cost. If keeping a minimum balance in your checking account costs you $5 a month in opportunity costs but saves you $7 in fees, it makes sense to go with that option.

Question 49: **Should I keep all my money in my checking account?**

If you have savings and checking accounts at the same bank, keep only as much money in the checking account as you need to pay bills that are due immediately. Let the rest of your funds go to work for you by earning interest in your savings account. When interest rates are very low, the earnings may be minimal, but when rates are higher, the savings can be substantial over time.

Question 50: **What is overdraft protection?**

Overdraft protection is a checking account feature that allows you to write checks for more than the balance in your account. It provides a safety net to protect you from accidentally overdrawing your account. Some banks allow you to cover overdrafts automatically from your savings account, money market account, or credit card account.

The most common method of covering overdrafts involves establishing a line of credit, which typically has an interest rate that can be as much as two times higher than the going rates on credit cards or loans. The cost to you could be substantial if you don't repay it right away. There can also be a fee each time funds are drawn from another source to cover your overdraft.

Question 51: **How can I avoid overdraft fees?**

Overdraft fees are one of the costliest banking mistakes you can make, and you should avoid them like the plague. Even if you don't balance your checkbook, at least compare your check register to your bank statement to make sure you've recorded all checks and ATM withdrawals and that the bank has properly credited you with all deposits. This will help prevent bouncing checks.

Typical fees for insufficient funds range from $20 to $35. Often when you bounce one check, at least one more check will bounce before you're aware of the problem, and before you know it you can rack up over $100 in bounced check fees.

If your overdraft protection is linked to your credit card, the bank issues a cash advance to cover your overdraft and charges it to your credit card. You pay a cash advance fee of 2 to 3 percent plus the fee your bank charges for the transaction, plus whatever interest you incur before you pay the cash advance back.

Question 52: **What should I do to minimize ATM fees?**

ATM fees are huge money generators for banks. Originally, ATMs were intended to reduce banks' expenses by automating tasks that previously involved a live teller. Now many banks charge fees for the use of ATMs.

There are several different types of ATM fees. Some banks charge you a fee just to have the use of an ATM card. Others charge ATM access fees, which are weekly, monthly, or yearly fees in addition to the regular account fees. When you use an ATM that is not owned by your bank, you'll incur a surcharge, which is a fee in addition to fees charged by your own bank, a practice called double dipping.

Establish an account at a bank with a large ATM network so you don't get stuck using out-of-network ATMs. Plan cash withdrawals when you can access your own bank's ATMs, or look for ATMs that don't impose a surcharge (usually indicated on the ATM). Double up transactions, like using your ATM card to get cash back when you make a purchase at a point-of-sale cash register. Avoid higher-cost ATMs found in convenience stores, hotels, casinos, restaurants, and airports.

Question 53: **What can I do to prevent identity theft?**

Debit cards that require a PIN are safer than those that require only a signature. If your card is lost or stolen, anyone can sign your name, but a thief can't use your PIN-based debit card unless he or she has your PIN. If you have a card that allows both types of transactions, a thief could use your card even without your PIN.

Don't leave your receipts behind when you use your debit card or throw them away without shredding them. Thieves who "dumpster-dive" may find your receipt and use the personal information on it to rip you off. Never write your PIN on your debit card or share your PIN with somebody else. Don't use a PIN that is too obvious, such as your phone number or birth date.

Beware of skimming devices posing as ATMs. They record electronically stored information from the magnetic strip of your card or your PIN as you enter it. The thieves then skim money from your bank account. Stick to bank ATMs instead of those in malls, airports, and other public places.

Question 54: **If someone steals my debit card, will I be responsible for the thief's charges?**

If you notice a transaction on your statement that isn't legitimate, report it immediately. If you report it within sixty days, your liability is capped at $500, but if you wait more than sixty days, you're liable for everything the thief removes from your checking account and your overdraft account, if you have one. This is another reason to review your bank statement each month.

Visa and MasterCard have voluntarily extended the same protection to customers using deferred debit cards as they offer to credit card customers: Your liability is capped at $50 if you report the card missing within two days. However, this feature was instituted voluntarily by Visa/MasterCard and doesn't have the force of law, so it could change at any time.

Question 55: **What's the best way to confirm that the bank has not made any errors on my accounts?**

Balancing your checkbook is a method of verifying that your records (your checkbook register) match the bank's records, as shown on your monthly bank statement. The method of accomplishing this task is changing in the electronic age, with the use of online banking and personal-finance software, but the pencil-and-paper method still works. The best time to balance your checkbook is within a few days of receiving your monthly bank statement so there are fewer transactions to wade through.

You have sixty days to inform the bank of any errors on your statement (and banks DO make errors). If you don't balance your checkbook monthly, how will you find an error if it does occur? Of course, it's much more likely that you made an error when recording a check or deposit or when adding or subtracting amounts in your checkbook register. You're unlikely to find your own errors unless you balance your checkbook each month or start bouncing checks, an expensive way to find out you made a mistake.

Question 56: **Aside from a savings account, what is a better option for protecting and growing my savings?**

Savings often end up sitting in the checking account just because it's the easiest option. It's not a good idea, though. Savings should be segregated from your day-to-day spending money for several reasons, including the fact that it's much too easy to dip into your savings if they're mingled with your checking account. You'll also earn better interest in a nonchecking account.

Money market deposit accounts, offered by most banks, are also FDIC-insured. They usually require a minimum balance of $1,000 or more, but they pay slightly higher interest rates than traditional savings accounts.

Be aware of the difference between money market deposit accounts offered by your bank and money market funds offered by brokerages and mutual fund companies, which are not FDIC-insured. These funds are typically invested in safe securities like government bonds and CDs, but their value is not guaranteed.

Question 57: **What is a CD?**

Certificates of Deposit (CDs) are actually loans you make to the bank for an agreed-upon term in return for a guaranteed interest rate on your principal. Some have adjustable rates tied to an index like Standard & Poor's 500 stock index. Most CDs charge a penalty if you withdraw all or part of your funds before the maturity date. Like other bank accounts, CDs are insured up to $100,000 as long as the bank is FDIC-insured. The $100,000 refers to the total of your accounts with that particular bank, so if you have more than $100,000 in one bank, you're not fully protected.

Question 58: **Should I put my money into a CD?**

CD terms range from one month to five years or more. The longer the term, the higher the interest rate and the greater the risk that your money will be locked up at a lower rate when interest rates rise. As with any investment, you have to balance the risk with the reward and make a decision within your comfort level.

Banks and brokers also offer callable CDs with rates that may seem too good to pass up, but be sure to read the fine print and ask plenty of questions before investing in a callable CD. Usually the issuer has the right to call the CD at any time after one year, but this doesn't mean it matures in one year. It may be a twenty-year CD, which means you can't cash it in without a penalty for twenty years, but the bank can call the CD at any time.

If interest rates have risen since the CD was issued, the bank will keep the CD in force because the rate will be below the current market rates. If interest rates have fallen, the bank will call the CD so it doesn't have to pay you above-market rates. This leaves you with money to invest at low rates when you may have thought you were locked in at a higher rate for a longer period.

Read the fine print very carefully when investing in a callable CD and be sure you know the difference between the maturity date and the callable date.

PART **II**

Managing Debt

Chapter 5

TACKLING STUDENT LOANS

IF YOU'RE ONE of the 60 to 67 percent of college graduates with student loans, there's a lot you need to know about repayment and how to keep your interest costs as low as possible. If the thought of paying off the large balances seems overwhelming, or if you're struggling to make the payments, you have options available to you to make it easier. If you're one of the millions of Americans who were able to attend college thanks to the availability of federally insured student loans, you have a responsibility to be informed about the repayment process. You're liable for your student loans even if you don't graduate, or if you graduate but can't find employment.

Question 59: **Once I'm out of school, when do I have to start repaying my loans?**

The day after you graduate, withdraw, or drop to less than halftime status, your six-month grace period begins (some types of loans have different grace periods). You're allowed one grace period per loan, during which no principal payments are required. Your first loan payment will be due approximately thirty to forty-five days after the end of your grace period.

Be sure to notify your lender of your current address, so they can contact you during your grace period to let you know the amount of your monthly payment, the payment due dates, how long it will take you to repay your loans, and the current interest rate.

Question 60: **How can I qualify for a deferment?**

Deferment is one option for relief during a period of financial difficulty. If you qualify for a loan deferment, you won't be required to make principal payments on your loan during that period.

You can qualify for a deferment under the following circumstances:

- Unemployment
- Enrollment in school
- Graduate fellowship
- Financial hardship
- Rehabilitation program due to disability

Question 61: **What options do I have if I can't get a deferment?**

If you don't qualify for a deferment, you may qualify for forbearance, a special arrangement with your lender that allows you to reduce or postpone principal payments temporarily. Interest continues to accrue during this period on both subsidized and unsubsidized Stafford loans, and if you don't pay it during the forbearance, it will be added to the balance of your loan. This costs you more in the long run because you'll be paying interest on the interest.

Question 62: **What can I do to qualify for a forbearance?**

You can automatically receive a forbearance if you participate in a qualifying program such as a medical or dental internship or residency, AmeriCorps, or if you're serving on active duty as a member of the U.S. armed forces. You may also qualify for debt-burden forbearance if your student loan payments are high compared to your income. Other forbearances are granted at the discretion of the lender based on your individual circumstances.

To request a deferment or forbearance, you have to complete an application available from your lender. Some lenders provide these online. Within thirty days of submitting your application, you'll be notified in writing whether or not your deferment or forbearance was approved.

Question 63: **When deciding on a repayment plan, should I just choose the one with the lowest monthly payment?**

If you're trying to minimize your monthly payment, try to balance your immediate need for lower payments with your long-term financial goals, which include paying off debt at the lowest reasonable cost. Review the status of your student loans annually to see if you're taking advantage of all the benefits offered by lenders and if the plan you're in still suits your changing financial situation. Just because the terms of your student loans include a particular repayment plan doesn't mean you're stuck with it; if it isn't working for you, you can apply for a change (you can even do it online). There are several options available:

1. Standard repayment: You pay the same amount each month over ten years or less, which results in lower interest costs than most other options, except prepayment.

2. Graduated repayment: You repay the loan over the same period but the payments are smaller in the early years and significantly larger in the later years. Because the lower payments include mostly interest and you don't pay the balance as quickly, you'll pay more interest.

3. Income sensitive or income contingent repayment: If you're eligible for these options, your payments can be based on a fixed percentage of your gross income each month. The percentage is between 4 and 25 percent and your payments are made over fifteen years with the income sensitive repayment plan and twenty-five years with the income contingent repayment plan. You have to reapply every year.

4. Extended repayment: This plan gives you lower monthly payments over a twelve- to thirty-year period using either the standard or graduated repayment plans if you owe more than $30,000 in federal student loans.

5. Loan consolidation: This option allows you to combine all of your eligible student loans into one loan with one monthly payment.

6. Prepayment: No matter what plan you have, there's always the option of prepaying all or part of your student loans at any time without penalty, which can greatly reduce your interest costs.

Question 64: **Is it possible to have my loans forgiven altogether?**

In limited circumstances, some student loans can be forgiven without requiring repayment. You may be eligible to have part of your Stafford loan canceled if you obtained it on or after October 1, 1998 and you've taught full-time for five years in a low-income school. You can obtain an application from your student loan lender.

For more information on the loan forgiveness program for child care providers, call 1-888-562-4639 or write to the Child

Care Provider Loan Forgiveness Program, P.O. Box 4639, Utica, NY 13504. For information on the nursing forgiveness program, call NELRP toll-free at 1-866-813-3753.

Question 65: **What is a Stafford loan?**

The most common type of student loan is a Stafford loan. These are either subsidized, meaning that the federal government pays the interest while you're in school and during grace and deferment periods, or unsubsidized, which means you're responsible for interest during these periods. Stafford loans first disbursed on or after July 1, 1995 have a variable interest rate, which changes on July 1 of each year based on Treasury bill rates, but can never exceed 8.25 percent. Rates as of July 2002 were the lowest in the history of the student loan program: 4.06 percent for Stafford loans and 4.86 percent for PLUS loans (loans to parents).

Stafford loans obtained through lenders associated with Sallie Mae, the largest education finance company in the United States, may be eligible for decreased interest rates if the first forty-eight payments are made on time. Consider having payments automatically deducted from your checking account each month to ensure you're not late with a payment.

If you don't have a Sallie Mae loan, consider transferring your loan or refinancing it with a Sallie Mae lender to take advantage of Sallie Mae's incentives, like the interest reduction. Other lenders may offer similar rewards. When rates are low, you can take advantage of the opportunity to pay off your loans more quickly by continuing to make the higher payments even though your required payment is lower.

Question 66: **How is a federal Perkins loan different from other loans?**

Most students need a combination of several different types of financial aid to pay for their education. When Stafford loans and other financial sources aren't sufficient to cover costs, Perkins loans are sometimes available.

The college decides on the amount of the loan, up to $4,000 per year for undergraduate students, with a maximum of $20,000 if you've completed two years of undergraduate study, or $8,000 if you've completed less than two years of undergraduate study. Graduate students can borrow a maximum of $6,000 for each year of graduate or professional study, up to a maximum of $40,000, including any undergraduate Perkins loans. Although these are the maximum amounts allowed by law, actual awards are usually less because schools try to use their limited funds to assist as many eligible students as possible.

Colleges award federal Perkins loans as part of their financial aid programs, based on financial need. The federal government provides most of the funds and the college kicks in the rest. Interest rates are fixed at 5 percent for the life of the loan, which cannot exceed ten years. No interest payments are required while you're a student, as long as you attend at least half time. There's a nine-month grace period, and repayment is made directly to the college.

Question 67: **Can I defer my Perkins loan?**

You may be able to receive a deferment or forbearance on a Perkins loan by applying to your college. During a deferment, you can temporarily postpone payments without accruing interest. If you're not eligible for a deferment, you may qualify for a forbearance, which allows you to reduce or postpone payments for a limited period of time. Interest will accrue during this period and you'll be responsible for paying it.

Part of your Perkins loan may be forgiven or canceled if you work full-time in certain occupations. For example, you may be eligible for loan cancellation if you teach full-time at a low-income school or in certain subject areas where there's a teacher shortage. See the financial aid officer at your college for details about the occupations that may qualify you for loan cancellation.

Question 68: **Is there any reason why I shouldn't take a deferment or forbearance if I qualify for one?**

The sooner you start paying off your loans and the larger your monthly payment, the less your loans will cost you in the long run. It may be difficult for the first few years to pay more than the minimum, especially if your loans are very large or your income is very low. If you find yourself having difficulty making your loan payments, it's better to be proactive than to make late payments or default on your loans.

Question 69: **What if I can't make the payments on my student loan?**

Student loans are the first real debt many people incur. Late payments or defaults can seriously harm your credit record for many years, but if you pay on time you can build a positive credit history that will help you qualify for a home mortgage, new car loan, or other type of credit. The federal government has made it increasingly difficult to escape your student loan debt, and there is no statute of limitations, so you can be sure it will dog you forever if you don't pay.

If you're having trouble making your loan payments, you have several alternatives. You could change your repayment plan, apply for deferment or forbearance, or apply for a loan consolidation, which could reduce your monthly payments by nearly half. If you've tried everything and are still having problems with your loan, contact your borrower advocate, who can act as a liaison between you and your lender and may be able to help find solutions to your problem.

Question 70: **What does it mean to be "in default" of a loan?**

If you're late with a payment for 270 days, you'll be considered in default of your student loan. Once you're in default, your lender will file a default claim with the guaranty agency, which buys your account from the lender and assigns the loan to a collection agency. The government also notifies all the credit bureaus.

Sometimes default information doesn't get removed from credit histories, even though the law requires it. Wait two or three months after you've made your twelfth on-time payment to rehabilitate your loan, then order a copy of your credit report to ensure that the negative information has been removed.

Question 71: **How would defaulting on my student loan affect me?**

If you don't pay your defaulted loan right away, you could have your federal income tax refunds withheld and applied to the loan balance, your wages garnished, collection costs of up to 40 percent of the loan levied against you, and face possible legal action. If you have a professional license or certificate of any kind (medical, law, accounting, and so on), it could be revoked. You may no longer be eligible for federal financial aid programs. You also lose your eligibility for federal loans like FHA and VA loans, which enable many people to buy a house that they wouldn't qualify for otherwise, and you may be denied credit cards or other forms of credit.

The default will show up on your credit report for seven years and could affect your ability to rent a house or apartment, buy a car, qualify for a mortgage, or even find a job. In the long run, it will cost you much less if you make your payments on time. Collection costs that are charged to you could total nearly half your balance, plus there's a 28 percent commission charged by the collection agency and that gets passed on to you. The government may even sue you and take your car, bank accounts, and other valuable property that you own and place a lien on your house, if you own one.

Question 72: **What can I do to minimize the damage after I've defaulted on my loan?**

Once you've defaulted on your student loans, any unpaid interest is computed and the entire balance of the loan becomes due and payable immediately. Once you reach this point, you have several options to avoid the negative consequences of default:

* You can pay off your entire student loan in one lump sum.
* You can establish monthly payment arrangements with your guaranty or collection agency (rehabilitation).
* You can consolidate your account into one new loan.

When you come to a repayment agreement with your lender, guaranty agency, or collection agency, a new loan is created that wipes out the old, defaulted loan.

Rehabilitation is a federal repayment program offered to student loan holders who have defaulted on their loans. To rehabilitate your loan, you have to make twelve on-time monthly payments in a row. Then the government agrees to once again insure your loan and your guaranty agency can sell it to a secondary market or lender, removing it from default status. After making twelve on-time payments, apply for rehabilitation. Once your loan has been rehabilitated, you have up to nine more years to repay it.

Question 73: **Should I consolidate my student loans?**

If you have several loans, you may want to consolidate them after you graduate just to simplify your record keeping and bill paying or to take advantage of lower interest rates or the longer repayment period you get from consolidating. Consolidating may be a good option for you if you have heavy education debt, want to lock in at a fixed rate, or want to reduce your monthly payments and are willing to pay more over the length of your loan in order to do so.

Under the Federal Consolidation Loan Program, if you owe $7,500 or more in eligible federal student loans and you're not in default on any of them, you can consolidate your loans at a fixed interest rate with only one payment a month. The interest rate on consolidation loans is an average of the interest rates on all your student loans, not to exceed 8.25 percent, so you may benefit from locking in when the current rate is very low. It could save you thousands of dollars over the life of your loans, depending on how much you owe.

The federal program also allows you to extend the term of the loan up to thirty years. Obviously a loan period this long would cost you much more in interest, but there are no prepayment penalties, so you can always pay more or pay the loan off early. Before you extend your loan repayment period, use an online calculator to calculate the true cost over time.

Chapter 6

HANDLING CREDIT CARDS

THERE'S NO QUESTION about it: Credit cards are a wonderful convenience that can make your life easier. However, if you overuse them, they're also the biggest deterrent to reaching your financial goals. To avoid this you need to have an understanding of how credit cards really work and how they can work in your favor.

With credit cards, you don't have to carry cash or your checkbook around with you. You can make purchases over the telephone or the Internet. You can reserve cars and hotel rooms, or have recurring expenses automatically billed to your card. You can buy things you need that you once would have had to wait years to obtain while you saved your money. You can cover unexpected large expenses like major auto repairs that once may have thrown you into a tailspin.

But the same cards that provide great convenience may become the means by which you are enslaved to debt, as charges you make become grossly inflated by high interest rates. As your debt grows out of control, it may even outlast the purchases that created the debt in the first place.

Question 74: **What's the definition of a credit card?**

Before you accept one or more of those preapproved credit card offers you find in your mailbox, make sure you understand the distinction between the different types of credit cards and the terms and conditions that will affect your costs. There are several types of plastic cards that are loosely referred to as credit cards, but they don't all work alike. Bankcards include Visa, MasterCard, and Discover. These card companies allow you to make purchases up to a preset credit limit ranging from $500 to $10,000 or more, depending on your income and credit history. You can pay the balance in full each month, the minimum required by the card company, or any amount in between.

Gold and platinum cards are cards that include extra perks such as collision coverage when you rent a car, extended warranties beyond the manufacturer's warranty on certain items, travel insurance, discounts, and other benefits. They sound appealing, but consider what exactly you get for the privilege of paying a much higher annual fee.

Question 75: **What are some of the costs of having credit cards?**

There are several types of costs associated with credit cards. The annual fee is a flat dollar amount the issuer charges each year for the use of the card. Many, but not all, issuers charge annual fees, so look for no-fee credit cards (but be sure to consider all the other factors such as grace period, interest rate, and so on). Finance charges are calculated based on the interest rate your card issuer charges and are the main cost of using credit. These rates vary significantly from one card to another, so you can save a lot of money by shopping around for a card with a lower interest rate. Other fees that you might incur on your credit card include application fees, processing fees, charges for exceeding your credit limit, late-payment fees, balance transfer fees, credit life insurance, and fees on cash advances.

Question 76: **What should I look for when choosing a credit card?**

If you pay the balance every month, the annual fee and other charges may be more important than the annual percentage rate (APR), so you should look for a no-fee or low-fee card. If you carry a balance and pay for your purchases over time, the APR and the method of computing your balance are most important, so you'll want to look for the lowest interest rate and the best grace period.

Beware of teaser rates, which sound tempting because the introductory rate is much lower than the going rate on most cards. The downside is that if you have a balance on the card when the introductory rate ends, you could be in worse shape than you were with a higher rate, depending on how high the rate spikes at the end of the introductory offer.

Question 77: **Should I choose a card that gives me frequent flier miles or cash back on my purchases?**

Getting a rebate or frequent flier miles is usually not a good reason to choose one card over another unless everything else is equal. You'd have to do a lot of flying to build up enough frequent flier miles to pay for the fee that often accompanies these cards.

Interest rates on cards that award frequent flier miles for certain purchases are usually several percentage points higher than regular credit cards, so don't carry a balance on them. If you pay even one day late, you're hit with finance charges and you may lose any miles earned that month.

Question 78: **What kind of interest rate should I be paying?**

In general, if you have a good credit history and you're paying more than 7 or 8 percent above the current prime interest rate, you're paying too much. When the prime rate is in the single digits, for example, lenders that charge 16 to 21 percent interest on credit card balances are gouging you. A few percentage points in the interest rate could save you thousands of dollars depending on your balance and how quickly you pay it off.

If you can obtain a lower-interest credit card, you can usually use cash advances to pay off the balance on your other credit cards and transfer this debt to the lower-rate card. Be sure to read the fine print, though. The interest rate on cash advances and transferred balances is usually much higher than the standard interest rate, so be sure you can pay off the cash advance before the introductory offer runs out.

If you have a questionable credit history, you'll pay higher interest rates. Lenders try to reduce their risk by increasing the interest charges on higher-risk debts. The higher the rate, the faster your debt will grow, and the harder it will be for you to pay it off.

Question 79: **Can I get a credit card even if I have damaged credit?**

Sometimes people make unwise choices or take on more credit than they can handle and end up with a bad credit history. Sometimes they acquire bad credit through divorce, loss of a spouse, or bankruptcy. If you have bad credit, or have no credit history, chances are you can still get a credit card, but it will cost you more, and the terms won't be as favorable as they are for those with good credit or a history of making timely payments. You may only be able to get a $500 credit limit, and you'll probably pay an exorbitant interest rate. Use the card wisely and make your payments on time, and eventually you'll qualify for better terms.

Question 80: **What should I consider when applying for credit cards?**

Research the best credit card deals, and apply only to one at a time. Applications for credit show up on your credit report and can make potential credit card issuers nervous, because they think you may be taking on more credit than you can handle. If you get turned down for a major credit card, try a department store card or gas card. These are often easier to get and making your payments on time for one of these cards can build a credit history that will help you qualify at some point for a major credit card.

Question 81: **What is a secured credit card?**

You put your own money into a savings account and that amount, or some portion of it, becomes the security for your credit line. If you don't pay your bills, the card issuer will use the money from your savings account to cover your debt. You can build a credit history using this method. Many people find that after twelve to eighteen months of making timely payments on a secured card, they can "graduate" to a regular credit card.

As with any credit card offer, beware of disreputable issuers. Secured cards are a favorite with unscrupulous marketers and you're a potential target because you can't easily obtain credit. Study the fine print before applying. Secured cards typically carry a higher interest rate and higher fees. Ask whether there are application or processing fees, which can total hundreds of dollars. The latest trend in secured cards is no application fees, so do your homework and save yourself some money.

Question 82: **Should I take advantage of the cash advances my credit card company offers me?**

Cash advances on a credit card come with a price tag—very high interest rates and fees. This feature is for the true emergency, not for buying nonessentials. If you're using cash advances for nonemergencies like eating out, paying your regular bills, or for entertainment or vacations, run to your nearest credit-counseling agency.

Grace periods don't apply to cash advances, so you pay interest from the day you get the cash. There's also usually a transaction fee of anywhere between 2 and 3 percent of the cash advance total. To add insult to injury, the interest rate on cash advances is significantly higher than the rate on purchases. All in all, your cash advance can end up costing you a bundle of money.

Visa cardholders take out a staggering $100 billion a year in cash advances. At an average up-front fee of 3 percent, cash advances are generating $3 billion a year to Visa in this type of fee alone.

Question 83: **What is a credit report?**

If you want to get out of credit card debt without falling victim to fraud and credit repair scams, you need to know what's on your credit report and why it's there, develop a plan to pay down debt, and change the way you use credit to avoid repeating the same problems.

The first step is finding out what your creditors are saying about you. A credit report is a record of your credit payment history as reported to credit bureaus by your bank, credit card companies, department stores, and other businesses you've borrowed from. Potential lenders use the information in your credit report to decide whether they want to take the risk of issuing you credit. If you understand how credit reports work, you can protect your rights and avoid being taken advantage of by unscrupulous credit repair clinics and so-called credit doctors.

Question 84: **Why do I need to know what's on my credit report?**

If you're thinking about buying a house or applying for credit for any other big purchase, you'll need a good credit report. It's always best to know what's on it before your lender does, so you'll have an opportunity to clean up any discrepancies or errors. You should also cancel any unused credit cards so the lender won't include your credit limit in your total debt. Lenders consider how much potential debt you have, not just how much you have outstanding on your credit cards and other loans. If you have credit cards with no balance but with credit limits totaling $4,000, for example, the lender will consider it an additional $4,000 in debt, and will reduce the amount of the loan they're willing to give you.

Question 85: **Why should I make more than the minimum monthly payment every month?**

The minimum monthly payment for most credit card companies is around 2 percent of the balance, including interest. If you made a purchase of $2,500 at an annual interest rate of 18 percent, it would take you almost twenty-eight years to pay off the balance by making the minimum monthly payment. Initially, 2 percent of your balance would be a minimum payment of $50.00, with around 75 percent, or $37.50, going toward interest and only 25 percent, or $12.50, reducing the amount you borrowed. You can see why it would take so many years to pay off your balance.

By the time you paid off the $2,500, you'd end up paying interest of $5,896 in addition to the $2,500 principal you borrowed. Your $2,500 item will have cost you $8,396. How can you ever get ahead financially if you're paying such exorbitant prices? Next time you're tempted to use your credit card, think about the real cost of the item you're buying. You wouldn't pay $8,396 for an item that is clearly marked with a $2,500 price tag, would you? That's exactly the type of inflated price you're paying when you make only the minimum payment each month on a credit card with an interest rate in the teens.

Question 86: **If I have too much credit card debt, how can I start to pay it off?**

First, to really get a handle on your debt, develop a written plan. Prepare a schedule of your debts, listing the creditor, the balance due, the interest rate, and the current monthly payment. Rank the debts in descending order by interest rate (highest interest rate first, lowest interest rate last). Each month, pay the minimum balance on all credit cards except the one with the highest interest rate. Pay as much as you possibly can on this card each month until it's paid off. Use all available money for this payment including overtime pay, tax refunds, bonuses, money generated by reducing expenses, and your bottle deposit money.

Question 87: **What should I do once I've paid off my credit card with the highest interest rate?**

Pause briefly to congratulate yourself, and then start in on the next debt with the highest interest rate. Pay as much as you possibly can each month, including the amount you were previously applying to debt number one. Continue to pay the minimum balance on the others. Keep moving down the list of debts until they're all paid off.

This is the only time you should ever pay the minimum balance on any credit card.

Question 88: **Should I use a credit counseling service to help pay off my debts?**

Nonprofit consumer credit counseling agencies may consolidate your debts into a single, manageable monthly bill. You pay the agency each month and they distribute the money to your creditors. This type of arrangement is not a consolidation loan, but it has its benefits because creditors will often accept lower payments if you're working with a reputable credit-counseling agency. Services may be free or provided for a very low fee of $10 to $15 a month.

Counselors are trained in helping consumers get out of debt and will work with you to get late fees waived and interest rates reduced. You may have to agree not to use credit and not to apply for new credit while you're participating in the debt repayment program.

Chapter 7

CONSIDERING CAR LOANS

BUYING A CAR is a big deal that can cost you big money. Whether you pay cash, lease, or finance your new car, there are pitfalls to steer clear of and information to gather to avoid paying too much. And maybe you should consider buying a used one, anyway. The Internet has revolutionized how we buy cars and made it possible for you to educate yourself before you head to the dealer.

When you're in the market for a car, the first step is deciding whether to buy new or used. If money is no object, you'll probably go for new. If you want to minimize the costs, you may decide to buy used. If it's important to you to have a new car or you're concerned about the potential problems with a used car, you may decide to buy the best new car you can afford even if money is tight. Either way, you can reduce your costs substantially if you arm yourself with the information included in this chapter.

Question 89: **Should I buy a new or a used car?**

As gratifying as it is to buy new, you can save a lot of money by buying a car that's one to three years old. That's because cars depreciate dramatically in the first two years—as much as 30 to 40 percent. The car that you paid $20,000 for just two short years ago may be worth only $12,000 now. If you plan to keep it for eight or ten years, it's a moot point, but if you like to trade cars every few years, it could cost you a lot of money.

The used cars of today are not the same as the used cars of yesterday. In general, today's cars are built better. Dealers and manufacturers now offer warranties on used cars that are in good condition, so you don't have to buy new to get quality.

Question 90: **I've found a used car I really like—what do I do next?**

There's always a chance with a used car that you're buying somebody else's problems. Once you've identified a used car you're interested in, play it safe and check out its history to make sure you're not buying a lemon. In just seconds, Carfax.com *(www.carfax.com)* will check its database of over two billion records and produce a report that reveals hidden problems that may affect the safety or resale value of the car. You may find that the car was turned in under the lemon law, salvaged after being totaled in an accident or flood, or used as a taxi. The report may reveal that the odometer was rolled back. To use this service, all you need is the vehicle identification number (VIN) of the car, usually found on a metal plate inside the windshield. The cost is $14.99 for a single report or $19.99 for unlimited reports for thirty days. The service is really worth the price—it could save you thousands of dollars and many headaches.

Question 91: **Should I trade my old car in to the dealership?**

You can really get fleeced when you trade your car in. You almost always come out ahead by selling your old car yourself. If you want to trade the car in, discuss the possibility only after you've already negotiated the best possible price for your new car. If you then decide to get a quote for a trade, you know there's no shuffling going on between the price of the new car and the trade-in amount.

Treat the trade-in and purchase of a new car as two separate transactions. Otherwise the dealer will make you believe he's giving you a good deal on the new car but will low-ball your trade-in, or will give you a good trade-in price but up the price of the new car.

Question 92: **What are my payment options when I want to buy a new or used car?**

When you're ready to buy a new car, you have three basic methods of paying for it: cash, loan, or lease. Most people don't walk into a dealership and plunk down $15,000 to $25,000 in cash for a new car, but if you're one of the few who are able to do this, or if you're financing part of the car but making a very large down payment, there's only one important factor you need to consider.

Paying cash will save you several thousand dollars in interest charges. But before you use your cash to avoid paying 5 to 7 percent interest on a car loan, you should have all your credit card or revolving credit loans paid off. It doesn't make sense to use cash if you have credit cards with higher interest rates than those of new car loans.

Most people finance the car through the dealer or their own bank and make monthly payments. The car is collateral for the loan, meaning that if you miss a payment, the lender can repossess it. The typical car loan used to be three years, but five-year loans have become very common. This makes a new car more affordable because the payments are spread out over a longer period, but it also costs more in interest charges.

Question 93: **How is a lease different from a loan?**

A lease is like borrowing a car rather than buying it. You make monthly payments for the period of the lease, usually three to five years. At the end of the lease term, you have the choice of returning the car to the dealer, buying it, or in some cases, renting it from month to month. Even though you don't own the leased car, you're responsible for insurance and regular maintenance and repairs not covered by the warranty. You'll be required to keep detailed records of service and repairs and will probably be required to have all services performed at the dealership where you bought the car or another dealership of the same manufacturer. If you lease only for the length of the warranty, you'll never have to pay for major repairs.

When you lease, you're paying only for a portion of the car's value, the part you "use up," known as depreciation. In a closed-end lease (a lease with a specific term), the price you'd pay to buy the car at the end of the lease is determined ahead of time. In an open-end lease, the car is priced at the end of the lease based on market value and the condition of the car.

Question 94: **When should I consider leasing instead of buying?**

One of the major attractions of leases is the lower cost. They require relatively little cash upfront, usually $500 plus one month's payment as a security deposit and the first month's payment on the lease. Instead of the sales tax being paid upfront like it is in new-car loans, a portion of it is paid each month. If sales tax in your state is 5 percent, the sales tax on a $20,000 car is $1,000. If you lease, that's $1,000 you don't have to borrow or cough up all at once.

Leasing may be a good option for you in two situations: you like to have a new car every few years and don't want to incur the costs of buying and selling, or you don't have the money to come up with a down payment on a new car.

Question 95: **What are the disadvantages of leasing?**

Leases may not be a good option for you if you put more than 12,000 to 15,000 miles per year on your vehicles. All leases include a mileage allowance, usually between 12,000 and 15,000 miles per year. If you exceed the allowance, you'll have to pay a fee at the end of the lease (often between ten and twenty cents per mile), which can add up to a significant amount of money. If your lease allows 12,000 miles per year and you average 14,000 per year for four years, the 8,000 extra miles at twenty cents per mile would cost you $1,600 in addition to your lease payments.

Leases can be confusing and most people enter into them without understanding how they work. As a result, they may end up paying far more than they should. Read all the fine print and ask questions to be sure you understand what you're getting into.

Question 96: **How can I save money when buying a new car?**

Once you've determined what car you want to buy, call around to several dealers and ask for their best price. Compare their estimates to information found on websites like Edmunds.com or Autobytel. com. Armed with this information and the true dealer's cost of the car and each option, you're ready to head to the dealership to begin your negotiations. The more information you have and the more you know about how new-car pricing and selling works, the better off you'll be.

Car-buying services like those offered by Costco (*www .costco.com*) and Autoweb.com (*www.autoweb.com*) negotiate special member-only prices with dealerships all over the country. You can research the cars you're interested in on Costco's website, do side-by-side comparisons of different models, set up an appointment at a participating dealership, and automatically get the no-haggle price if you're a Costco member. AutoWeb.com and other car-buying services work in similar ways.

Question 97: **How do I negotiate the price with the car dealer?**

It's surprising how many people walk into a dealership and pay the quoted price for a new car without attempting to negotiate. If you're one of those people, dealers will love to see you coming. They expect you to negotiate and will gladly pocket the profit when you don't.

There are two main keys to negotiating a price on a new car. The first is to keep the purchase, your trade-in, and the financing as three totally separate transactions. The second is to start with the invoice price (the dealer's cost) instead of trying to chip away at the manufacturer's suggested retail price (MSRP). Starting at the invoice price, subtract any manufacturer's rebates that you found on Edmunds.com to get the real dealer's cost (include rebates the dealer receives from the manufacturer but doesn't pass on to you). Make an offer of 5 percent above that and don't allow yourself to be pressured into paying more.

The dealer profit on options is higher than the profit on the base car, so there's more room to negotiate on options. You should go to the dealership armed with information on dealer cost not only for the car, but also for any options you're thinking of adding.

Question 98: **Aside from the initial price, what else should I consider when buying a new car?**

Try to look at the cost of ownership over a five-year period. Edmunds.com provides information on the true cost of ownership for many models, broken down by depreciation, financing, insurance, taxes and fees, fuel, maintenance, and repairs. Consider how quickly the car depreciates, or declines in value, by looking up the current *Kelley Blue Book (www.kbb.com)* value of a five-year-old car of the same or similar model.

You may be tempted by the looks of certain cars or trucks, or the affordable price of a particular model, but there's more to consider than appearances and cost when buying a new car. What's the repair record of this make and model? Are there problems with certain components of the car, like the brakes or the transmission? What does it cost for routine repairs and maintenance? What does it cost to insure? How is its safety record? These are all things you should know before you visit the dealership, especially if costs are important to you.

Question 99: **How do I know how much I will be paying in insurance?**

You may not have given much thought to how auto insurance rates are calculated, but the make and model of the car you buy can have a significant impact on the cost of your auto insurance. Some models are much more expensive to repair than others if they're damaged in an accident. Some models are more likely to be stolen. Insurance companies factor these things into their calculations in addition to such things as the city and state the car will be used in, how much mileage you expect to put on it each year, your driving record, and your claim history.

Even the color of your car can affect your insurance rates. For instance, red sports cars cost more to insure because insurance companies assume drivers of red sports cars will drive at excessive speeds and therefore get in more accidents.

Question 100: **Should I take the dealer's offer of an extended warranty?**

When you buy a new car you'll be offered an auto service contract to help protect you against the expense of major repairs. If the dealer tells you that your lender requires you to purchase an auto service contract to qualify for financing, call the lender directly to verify this. Prices on service plans vary greatly and you'll almost always pay much more if you buy it through the dealer. Read the contract carefully and make sure you're not duplicating coverage that's already offered by the manufacturer. Most new cars come with at least a one-year, 12,000-mile warranty, and some come with a three-year or 36,000-mile warranty. Any service plan you buy should kick in after the manufacturer's warranty runs out, or "wrap around" the manufacturer's warranty. Otherwise you're paying for duplicate coverage.

You'll need to know what repairs are covered (some plans explicitly disallow certain items or repairs), how long the contract lasts, whether repairs must be made by a certain company, and whether parts and labor are included. Most dealer plans are mechanical breakdown plans, not wear-and-tear plans. They cover only things that actually break, so something like piston rings that need to be replaced wouldn't be covered. You want a plan that includes both breakdowns and wear and tear.

Chapter 8

FILING FOR BANKRUPTCY

BANKRUPTCY IS A federal court process that places you under the protection of the bankruptcy court while you try to re-pay your debts (Chapter 13 bankruptcy) or removes the debts altogether (Chapter 7 bankruptcy). When you file for bank-ruptcy, an automatic stay goes into effect; the stay prohibits your creditors from attempting to collect the debt without the approval of the court, even if the bank is in the process of fore-closing on your house. Filing for Chapter 13 in this situation could buy you the time you need to sell the house yourself and pay off the mortgage.

Bankruptcy should not be entered into lightly. It has far-reaching effects on your ability to obtain credit, buy a house, buy life insurance, and sometimes even get a job. There are other factors that might make one type of bankruptcy better for you than another. Consult a good bankruptcy lawyer and provide all the details of your financial situation so he or she can counsel you concerning the option that best suits your needs.

Question 101: **What is Chapter 13 bankruptcy?**

Chapter 13 bankruptcy, which applies to most individuals, involves reorganization of your debts. You'll need to file a proposal with the bankruptcy court detailing your plan for repayment and include a detailed budget. Some debts can be erased altogether, others must be partially repaid, and others must be repaid in full. If your proposal is accepted, your wages will probably be garnished during the repayment period, which usually lasts three to five years. In Chapter 13 bankruptcy, you can prevent the loss of your home by immediately starting to make your regular mortgage payments and any catchup payments required by your repayment plan.

Question 102: **After I file for Chapter 13 bankruptcy, how much of my debts will I have to pay?**

The courts have discretion regarding how much of your debts you'll have to repay. Some courts don't require you to pay anything on debts that you aren't legally required to repay in full; others will want you to pay as much as possible. You may also be required to pay several years of interest on the total value of your nonexempt property to compensate creditors for the fact that they have to wait several years to be fully paid.

You must pay all of your missed payments on secured debt, like your house or car, if you want to keep the asset. The minimum amount you'll have to repay on your unsecured debt is the value of your nonexempt personal property. Each state has its own laws for determining nonexempt property, but in general, you'll be given an "allowance" that consists of several thousand dollars for a car, part of the equity in your home, necessary clothing, necessary household goods and furniture, appliances, and personal effects.

Question 103: **What debts will I still be responsible for after filing for bankruptcy?**

If you add up the equity in everything you own and deduct the amount of the exempt items, the difference is the least amount you'll owe. You'll have to pay more than this if you have nonexempt expenses like child support or back taxes.

Before you make the decision to file for bankruptcy, you should know which debts you may be able to walk away from and which you'll still be responsible for. Debts that can't be discharged or forgiven include child support and alimony, debts for personal injury or death caused by drunk driving, most student loans, traffic tickets and other fines or penalties imposed for breaking the law, certain types of taxes owed, and debts you forget to list in your bankruptcy papers.

Question 104: **How do I know if I'm eligible to file for Chapter 13 bankruptcy?**

Because repayment of some of your debts is the basis for this type of bankruptcy, you have to have regular income in order to be eligible. Regular income can include Social Security benefits, child care or alimony, and rental income, and, of course, employment or self-employment wages. You also have to have enough disposable income after your basic needs like housing, utilities, and food, to use for debt repayment. In addition, your secured debts (those with collateral, like a car or house) cannot exceed $871,550 and your unsecured debts (those with no collateral, like credit card debt, student loans, and medical bills) can't exceed $269,250.

Bankruptcy is considered the debt management tool of last resort because it has serious consequences. Since it stays in your credit history for ten years, it can affect your ability to obtain credit, a job, insurance, or housing.

Question 105: **How does Chapter 7 bankruptcy differ from Chapter 13 bankruptcy?**

Under Chapter 7, liquidation, you turn most of your personal property over to the court, which appoints a trustee to sell the property and use the proceeds to pay off all or some of your debts. As in Chapter 13 bankruptcy, you're allowed to keep certain exempt property, but to keep secured property such as your house, car, or furniture you're buying on credit, you have to sign a Reaffirmation Statement stating that you agree to be responsible for those debts.

Question 106: **What happens after I sign the Reaffirmation Statement?**

Once you've signed the Reaffirmation Statement, these debts can't be discharged for at least six years. In other words, you can't change your mind in a few years and decide you don't want those assets and don't want to be responsible for paying for them. In order to reaffirm the debt, you have to make any payments necessary to bring your account up to date.

Question 107: **How do I know if I should file for Chapter 7 bankruptcy?**

Chapter 7 is typically the bankruptcy type of choice for people who have large credit card or other unsecured debt and few assets. If there's a risk that you might lose your home or car under Chapter 7, your lawyer may recommend that you file Chapter 13 instead. If you have more equity in your car or home than the exempt amount allowed by your state, the chance of being forced to relinquish these assets to be sold to pay your creditors is high.

Question 108: **What debts will I have to repay under Chapter 7?**

Some debts may not be dischargeable in a Chapter 7 bankruptcy if a creditor challenges them. These include debts you incurred by fraud, like giving false information on a credit application; credit purchases over a certain amount in the sixty days prior to filing; loans or cash advances over a certain amount in the sixty days prior to filing; and debts you owe under a divorce settlement or decree, with certain exceptions.

A Chapter 7 bankruptcy stays in your credit history for ten years. During that period, you may be denied credit.

Question 109: **If I've incurred large debts that I cannot pay, can filing for bankruptcy help turn my life around?**

Filing for bankruptcy is not going to help you in the long run if you got there by irresponsible spending habits that you haven't changed. On the other hand, if job loss, high medical bills, disability, death, divorce, or other circumstances not entirely in your control have produced a financial burden you have no hope of getting out from under, bankruptcy may be the only way you can get a fresh start. The court will place restrictions on how you can spend money and will not allow you to buy what it considers nonessentials.

Question 110: **How can I avoid having to file for bankruptcy?**

If you find yourself falling behind on your bills, call your creditors immediately. Most will work with you if circumstances (job loss, divorce, illness, etc.) have made it temporarily difficult for you to meet your financial obligations. Suggest a temporary reduction in your payment, a waiver of late fees or penalties, skipping several payments now and increasing future payments to make up for it, or skipping several payments and adding them to the end of the loan.

Bankruptcy is not exactly a walk in the park. You won't automatically walk away debt-free. The ten-year period following the filing of bankruptcy may be difficult, as the bankruptcy follows you around whenever you apply for credit or even sometimes when you apply for a job. Before you resort to bankruptcy, there may be things you can do to improve your situation. If your debt isn't totally overwhelming, you may be able to cut back on nonessentials and find the money to apply to debt. You may even want to sell your car or house and buy a less expensive one. If you haven't taken advantage of the latest low mortgage rates, refinancing your mortgage (again) may net you a few hundred dollars a month that you could put towards your debt. As a last resort, you could apply for a hardship withdrawal from your 401(k) plan.

Question 111: **What should I do before I file for bankruptcy?**

You may feel hopelessly overwhelmed by your debt and see no way out from under it, but before you take a step as drastic as filing for bankruptcy, consider consulting with a reputable credit counselor. Debt Counselors of America and the National Foundation for Credit Counseling are the best known of these groups. Debt Counselors of America assists people over the Internet and by phone, while the NFCC has a national network of 1,450 offices called Consumer Credit Counseling Services. They provide counseling in person, as well as electronically. You don't have to be in dire straits to use this service. If you need help getting your financial affairs in order or setting financial priorities, give them a call.

Many creditors will accept reduced payments or give you time to catch up on late payments if you enter into a debt repayment plan with a reputable debt counseling organization. The counselor works with you to develop a payment schedule. You pay an agreed-upon amount to the organization monthly and they use it to pay your creditors. These services are free or very low cost. An important part of the plan is your agreement not to apply for any new credit or incur any additional debt while you're in the program.

Question 112: **If I want to avoid bankruptcy, can a credit repair clinic help?**

You're in debt up to your ears and along comes a credit repair clinic that promises to clean up your credit history in days. Why would you fall for this? Doesn't it sound too good to be true? Yet many people, desperate to resolve their credit and debt problems, pay these clinics large fees and walk away with nothing. It's always good to have a little healthy skepticism when evaluating any type of financial offer.

There's been an estimated $100 billion lost in illegal scams in the United States, ranging from illegal work-from-home employment scams to multilevel marketing scams, sweepstakes scams, telemarketing scams, fake charitable fundraising scams, credit repair scams, and many others.

Don't ever give your Social Security number, bank account number, or other personal financial information over the phone to someone you didn't call. No reputable company will require your Social Security number in order for you to claim a prize you won. Nobody needs your bank account number for any legitimate purpose. In fact, all a thief needs to call your bank and have money electronically transferred to his account as a "phone check" is your name and bank account number.

PART **III**

Getting
Established

Chapter 9

LAUNCHING YOUR CAREER

SALARY IS A very important factor in choosing a job, but it's not always the most important one. Evaluate the total compensation package: salary, insurance, paid leave, stock options, retirement plan, and other benefits. Once you've placed a dollar value on the employer-provided benefits, evaluate other aspects of the job, but remember that there are some things you can't put a price tag on, like training and experience. The best jobs will prepare you for the next step in your career by teaching you valuable skills and providing on-the-job training.

Knowing how to evaluate a prospective employer, determine your worth in the job market, negotiate the best salary and benefits, and request a raise will help you optimize job potential. In today's volatile market, it's equally important to know how to protect yourself financially if you lose your job.

Question 113: **Where can I learn more about a company I am interested in working for?**

How can you choose a job that has potential and doesn't end up being a dead end? When evaluating a potential employer, find out as much as you can about the industry. What's the history of growth in the industry and what's the anticipated future need for goods and services produced or provided by that industry? Is the industry trendy? Is it subject to government regulation? If so, what's the possible impact on the company?

Also find out as much as you can about the company or organization. Check for newspaper and magazine articles. Detailed information, including current financial information, is easily available at your local library or online if the company is publicly traded. Is the company financially stable? What are its size, reputation, and growth potential? How do the company's products or services compare to those of the competition? If you know anybody who has worked for the organization, find out what you can about the company culture and atmosphere and the quality of management.

Question 114: **How should I go about evaluating the job itself?**

Try to find answers to the following questions: Is there a training program or opportunity to obtain additional education? What are the day-to-day tasks and duties? What is the level of responsibility? Who will you report to and what is that person's leadership style?

What are your potential coworkers like? Does the job require travel, weekend work, or working long hours? What are the salary and benefits package? If the salary seems low, are there benefits that compensate for it?

Choosing a good organization and a good job can make a vital difference in your job satisfaction, opportunities for advancement, and salary potential. Do your homework in advance; it can pay off in both the short- and long-term.

Question 115: When I get a job offer, how will I know if the salary is reasonable?

Before you enter the job market, whether it's your first job out of college or a new step on your career path, you need to know what the going salary is in your geographical area for someone with your education, training, and skills. The U.S. Bureau of Labor Statistics (BLS) *Occupational Outlook Handbook* is an invaluable source of information on salaries in hundreds of different occupations. It also provides descriptions of what workers do on the job, working conditions, training and education needed, and expected job prospects in a wide range of occupations. In addition, the BLS provides information on wages, earnings, and benefits for many occupations by region, state, and metropolitan area. Visit BLS online at *www.bls.gov*.

Question 116: How can I make sure I'm getting the right salary and benefits package?

Much has been written about negotiating salary and benefits, but most of it boils down to knowing what you're worth in the marketplace, identifying which benefits are important to you, and putting a price tag on the benefits offered by your prospective employer so you can evaluate the real value of an offer. Total compensation encompasses much more than just salary.

When meeting with prospective employers, find out what benefits and perks the company pays employees in the position you're applying for, what an average pay increase is, and what benefits might be added to sweeten the pot if they're not able or willing to offer the salary you'd like.

Question 117: **When should I bring up the question of salary with my prospective employer?**

Experts caution job seekers to delay discussing salary until well into the interview process and to avoid telling interviewers your current salary. You shouldn't be pegged into a salary range that's lower than the going rate just because you're underpaid in your current job, and discussing salary too early in the process can stick you with a lower than acceptable offer or, conversely, take you out of the running if your current salary is too high. The goal is to have enough interaction with the interviewer to have a chance to sell yourself and convince her or him that you're the right person for the job before salary is discussed in any detail. The objective of asking your current salary or the salary you're looking for is usually to pay you as little as possible.

Question 118: **My new employer offers a flexible spending account to all employees. What is it and how does it work?**

Flexible spending accounts (FSAs), or reimbursement accounts, are an employer-provided benefit that allows you to set aside pretax contributions to pay for eligible medical expenses that aren't covered by your health insurance, including premiums (unless they're paid with pretax money), deductibles, copays, and any other health cost considered an allowable medical expense by the IRS. For a complete list of allowable medical deductions, see Publication 502, "Medical and Dental Expenses" in the Forms and Publications section of the IRS website at *www.irs.gov*, or request a printed copy of this publication from the IRS by calling 1-800-829-3676.

You benefit from an FSA because your contributions are deducted before taxes are calculated, thus reducing your taxes. Using the same tax brackets as the health insurance example, if your total tax percentage (federal, state, and Social Security) is 42.65 percent, every dollar you put into an FSA will cost you only fifty-seven cents. Don't contribute more than you think you'll use, because under IRS regulations, you forfeit any unused funds at the end of the year. If you have significant medical expenses you can save a lot of money, so don't overlook this great benefit.

Question 119: **I don't expect to retire for another thirty years or more. Should I start to contribute to my employer's retirement plan now?**

If your employer provides a 401(k) plan, you'd do well to participate—remember, your contributions are tax-deferred (except for Social Security taxes). If your employer matches a percentage of your contribution, add this to your compensation total when calculating the value of your benefits. Most employers match between fifty cents and $1 for every dollar you contribute, for up to 3 to 6 percent of your salary. If you earn $40,000 a year and contribute $200 a month and your employer match is 75 percent for up to 6 percent of your salary, your employer will kick in another $150 a month up to a maximum of $2,400 a year. Under this example, your employer is actually paying you an additional $1,800 a year ($150 × 12 = $1,800).

Question 120: **What are stock options?**

Stock option plans are a way for companies to share ownership with employees, reward them for performance, and attract, retain, and motivate staff. The days of average employees getting rich on stock options may be over, but stock options can still be a very worthwhile benefit. We've all heard lots of talk about stock options during the heyday of high-tech growth in the late 1990s, but few people really understand what they are and how they work.

A stock option gives an employee the right to buy company stock at a specified price during a specified period after the option has vested. Companies use the vesting period to motivate employees to stick around. Let's say you receive an option on 500 shares at $10 per share and the stock price goes up to $20. You can exercise the option and buy the 500 shares at $10 each, sell them for $20 each, and pocket the $5,000 difference. If the stock price never rises above the option price, you don't lose money but you don't make any, either. You simply don't exercise the option.

Question 121: **Should I participate in my company's employee stock ownership plan?**

Employee stock purchase plans (ESPPs) offer employees the chance to buy stock, usually through payroll deductions during an "offering period" at a discounted price. The employee can then sell it right away and take the profit created by the discount, or hold on to it in expectation that its value will increase.

Employee stock ownership plans (ESOPs) are a type of benefit plan, regulated by the federal government, in which a trust is set up to acquire some or all of the stock of the company and sell the stock to employees. Because ESOPs receive tax advantages, they're not allowed to discriminate in favor of key or highly compensated employees, so most employees get to participate. ESOPs are typically used as a type of retirement plan. Be cautious about investing the bulk of your retirement funds in company stock no matter how well established the company is. Take advantage of employee ownership but minimize your risk by putting most of your retirement money in other investments.

Question 122: **What are incentive stock options?**

Incentive stock options (ISOs) allow employees to purchase shares of stock at some time in the future at a specified price. The employee pays tax on the gain upon sale or disposition of the stock, not upon receipt or exercise of the option. Nonqualified stock options don't have the restrictions of other options and don't receive any special tax consideration. When employees exercise nonqualified options, they pay ordinary income tax on the difference between the grant price and exercise price.

Question 123: **How do I ask my employer for a raise?**

If you already have a job but feel underpaid, you may be thinking about asking your boss for a raise. If this is the case, you need to be prepared to convince the powers that be that you not only deserve one, but that you're worth it. Don't make the common mistake of basing your request on your need for more money or your inability to meet your financial obligations. Businesses do not base salary increases on employees' personal needs; they base it on employees' worth to the company, the quality of their work, company pay scales, and budgetary concerns. Need has nothing to do with it, so it's best not to talk about need when asking for a raise.

First, perform an evaluation of your skills, productivity, job tasks, and contribution to the company. Look at your job duties and performance from the company's perspective and base your approach on the company's needs. The goal is to show or remind your boss of your tangible contributions to the company, so make a list of your accomplishments, and if possible, the dollar value of each to the company.

Question 124: **How can I determine how much of a raise I should ask for?**

Determine the going rate, both inside and outside the company, for your job. Ask your company's human resources department for company salary ranges for your position and several related positions above yours. Review these, along with the salary information and compensation surveys from the Bureau of Labor Statistics' website. Be sure to consult some local information as well, by reading help-wanted ads or making a call to your local human resources organization, such as the Society for Human Resources Management (SHRM).

To increase your chances of getting the raise you want, you need to know several things about your company. What is the policy on salary increases? Are all employees reviewed at the same time each year? Does your department have a budget for salaries that they're required to stay within? If so, you're in direct competition with the other employees in your department for limited funds, and you should work on making yourself stand out above the crowd.

What is the company's financial condition? Are they struggling to stay afloat? Are they in a budget crisis? Perhaps it's been a good year and there's bonus money to be awarded to deserving employees, but no salary increases. The more you know about the company's financial situation regarding compensation, the better prepared you'll be for your salary negotiation.

Question 125: **When should I ask for a raise?**

Timing is everything. If you've only been at your job for a few months, asking for a raise probably won't go over very well. However, if you find after a few months that you were hired at a salary well below that of others in your position and with your experience, it may pay to discuss this with your supervisor. If you've been formally or informally disciplined or chastised recently, wait at least a few months before asking for more money.

The time of month, week, and day are also important. Don't ask to meet with your boss during the busiest time of the month or busiest days of the week, which for most people are Mondays and Fridays. It's to your advantage to arrange an appointment at a time that's convenient with your manager.

Question 126: **How do I know if I might be laid off?**

You may feel that your job is very secure and then walk in one day to be greeted by a pink slip. You don't need to be paranoid, but being prepared for the possibility of job loss will make it easier to deal with if it does happen. To be prepared, you need to know your net worth, set up a budget, save, and keep your debt low.

You should also have a feel for the stability of your job. How are your employer's competitors doing? Are they experiencing layoffs? Layoffs in your industry can be a good indication of the instability of your job, even if your employer has not yet made any cuts. If job layoffs have already occurred where you work, you should have your resume updated and be looking around for possible opportunities that fit your skills.

Question 127: **What should I do if I lose my job?**

If you get the pink slip, apply for unemployment on the first day of your layoff so you'll receive the maximum benefits for which you're eligible. Some people are reluctant to file for unemployment because they feel it's a type of welfare, but it isn't. Your employer contributes to your state's unemployment insurance fund as well as a federal unemployment fund. You earned those benefits by working. If you need them, use them.

Unemployment benefits are typically about half of your regular earnings, up to your state's cap, paid for a maximum of twenty-six weeks. You'll be required to prove that you're actively seeking work while receiving unemployment benefits, and you must be willing, available, and ready to work. Unemployment benefits are subject to federal income tax, so you'll need to claim them at the end of the year. Be prepared for the additional taxes you may owe as a result.

During a period of unemployment, resist the urge to use your credit cards unless absolutely necessary for critically important expenses. If you can't make ends meet, contact your creditors, tell them you've lost your job but are actively seeking employment, and request an arrangement that allows you to make reduced payments for a limited time. If you have a good credit history, they will probably be willing to work with you.

Chapter 10

RENTING AN APARTMENT

WHETHER YOU'RE LOOKING for a new place to live in the same town or moving to a new city for a job opportunity or change of scenery, there are financial issues to consider before you take the plunge. The more you know about the costs associated with your move, the better you can plan for the financial impact.

Take a few minutes to think about what's important to you in your living space before you start pounding the pavement looking for the perfect apartment. Make a list of the most important features like access to public transportation, being able to own pets, laundry facilities, a parking spot or availability of on-street parking, and the safety of the neighborhood. Identify the things you won't compromise on and those that would be nice but aren't absolute requirements. This will help you quickly rule out places that don't meet your minimum standards. If you can't find a suitable apartment in your price range, consider sharing a house or apartment with a roommate, or renting a studio or efficiency apartment.

Question 128: **How much can I afford to pay in rent?**

Before you start seriously shopping around for an apartment or rental house, you need to know how much you can afford to pay. As a general rule of thumb, allow no more than 30 percent of your gross income for housing. If you're making $35,000 a year, you shouldn't pay more than $875 a month for rent. You'd be more comfortable at 25 percent, or $729 a month. If some or all of the utilities are included, you could pay higher rent. You don't want to be strapped for cash all the time, so it's best to avoid the maximum you can afford.

Question 129: **Should I consider moving back home?**

There's a growing trend for young people to return to their parents' home for a few years after college graduation so they can save money before striking out on their own. If this option is acceptable to you and your parents, with discipline you could save a significant amount of money over the course of a year.

Let's say rentals in your area are $600 a month, and your parents will let you live at home rent-free as long as you contribute to household expenses like groceries and utilities. If you socked away what you'd be paying in rent living on your own, you could save

$7,200 plus interest in a year—not exactly small potatoes. You'd have to earn as much as $10,000 in order to net $7,200 after taxes.

Once you've experienced the freedom of being on your own in college you may find it difficult to move back in with your parents, so it's understandable if you just want to strike out on your own.

Question 130: **How can I find an apartment to rent?**

If you're looking in your own town, you probably know about some of the apartment complexes in your area. It's more difficult if you're moving to a new city, especially if you don't have the luxury of being able to go there to find housing before you move. A number of methods can make it easier.

If you know people in the area, ask around for recommendations. Word of mouth is invaluable. You'll learn important information that might not be readily apparent when you walk through the place, like noise levels, the safety of the neighborhood, and whether management is good about maintenance and repairs.

The local newspapers in most towns and cities advertise apartments for rent. Make a list of the ones that sound interesting and drive by to see if you want to look more closely at any of them. If you're familiar with the area, you'll be able to rule out some places upfront just by their address. If you're new to the area, be prepared to spend some time looking around.

Question 131: **Should I use a Realtor to help me find an apartment?**

Using a Realtor is a good idea if you're moving to a city that's unfamiliar to you. Another way to find Realtors with rentals is the Internet. Go to a good search engine and type in "real-estate agents" or "Realtors" and the name of the city and state. It may not be obvious from the description whether the Realtor does rentals, but a quick visit to the website will tell you. While you're searching, keep an eye out for real-estate agents who offer relocation packages with information about the city you're going to be living in. This could be helpful once you move.

Apartment finders or locators are companies that specialize in knowing all the apartment complexes in a given area. They work with apartment property managers to keep up to date on apartment availability, and save you the time and hassle of making phone calls to each individual complex to get information. Try to avoid using an apartment-finder service that costs money. Some of them charge an entire month's rent. There are many free apartment- and room-mate-finder services on the Internet, especially for larger cities, so you shouldn't have to pay for this service unless there's a severe rental shortage.

Question 132: **What should I consider when signing a lease?**

Four little words: Read the small print. Yes, it's boring, and it may not be the clearest writing you've ever read, but you have a lot at stake and you need to protect yourself by knowing all the rules and regulations of living in your new space and of leaving it. You don't want to end up trying to explain to Judge Judy that you signed a legally binding contract without even reading it.

If there are provisions in the lease that you object to, see if you can work out a compromise with the landlord. Cross out the unwanted language for any changes the two of you agree to, initial and date the change, and have the landlord do the same. Don't rely on oral agreements. They're difficult if not impossible to prove.

If there's something you don't understand, ask the landlord or property manager to explain it. Don't make any assumptions.

Question 133: **What if I need to leave before my lease ends?**

Getting out of your lease before the end of the lease term can be difficult and expensive. You can be held responsible for paying the rent for the remainder of the lease. Find out if there are circumstances that would release you from your obligation. What if you got a job transfer? Got divorced? Had a baby? Some landlords will allow you to break the lease for a fee. Others may allow you to sublet to another tenant.

Question 134: I don't want to commit to a one-year lease. Can I just rent on a month-to-month basis?

If you sign a month-to-month lease, be aware that the landlord can terminate the lease or raise the rent on short notice. Usually you're still obligated to give written notice of your intention to move out sixty days in advance. If you're not sure where you're going to be working or you intend to buy your own home after having a few months to get settled in a new town, a month-to-month lease might make sense for you.

Question 135: How can I make sure I get my security deposit back when I leave?

During the first week or so that you live in rented housing, go through every room and make a detailed list of everything that's broken, dirty, or damaged in any way, including chips in cabinets or tubs, holes in walls, broken windows, tears or stains on carpets, burns, and so on. If possible, take pictures of the damage. Send a copy of the list to your landlord and keep a copy with your pictures to use if needed.

Clean the apartment thoroughly before you move out (including carpets), and repair any damage you caused. Remove all of your belongings and any trash. Ask your landlord to walk through the apartment with you and give you a signed statement about the condition you left it in. This will be easier if you've already moved out your furniture. You may even want to take pictures of the condition of the apartment before you leave, in case you have to go to small claims court to get your security deposit back. Give the keys directly to the landlord (don't just leave them in the apartment) and leave your forwarding address so he or she can mail your deposit.

Question 136: **Will I have to pay to have my utilities (electricity, cable, etc.) turned on?**

You may be required to pay a refundable deposit and nonrefundable hookup charges to one or more utility companies, including electric, gas, water, sewer, and cable TV. Many electric companies require a deposit of several hundred dollars. If you can prove you had electric service recently in your name in another location and you had a good payment record, the utility company may waive this requirement. To prevent paying for utilities used by the previous tenant, if possible take utility readings as soon as you move in. (Ask your landlord how you can do this.) When you move out, be sure to request your deposit back from the utility company. Millions of dollars in unclaimed utility deposits sit in the coffers of state governments because residents moved without leaving a forwarding address.

Question 137: **Do I need to get renters' insurance?**

Most renters have the mistaken belief that they don't need renters' insurance. The building owner's coverage doesn't protect you against personal injury lawsuits if someone is injured in your apartment, and it doesn't protect you against damage that you or your guests cause to the property. If you overrun your bathtub and water leaks into the apartment below, you're liable for the costs, unless you have renters' insurance.

The building owner's coverage also doesn't provide for replacement of your belongings if they're stolen or damaged by fire or water. Renters' insurance does all of this, and is well worth the cost.

Question 138: **How much insurance coverage do I need?**

Even if you don't have much furniture or large household appliances, you'd be surprised at how much your belongings would cost to replace. For starters, you probably have several thousand dollars' worth of clothing. Take a detailed room-by-room inventory of your belongings, write down a brief description of each item, and estimate what it would cost to replace it. Include clothes in your inventory.

Question 139: **What's the difference between replacement cost and actual cash value?**

It's a good idea to buy coverage for replacement cost rather than actual cash value. Replacement cost coverage is just what it sounds like: if something you own is stolen or damaged by fire or water, the insurance company will pay you what it will cost to replace it with an item of similar quality. Actual cost value coverage assumes that your belongings lose value with time and usage, and pays you only the depreciated value of the items.

Note that you take big risks with actual cash value insurance. If you have stereo equipment that you paid $1,500 for and would now cost $2,000 to replace, you would be reimbursed $2,000 *minus* the insurance company's calculation for depreciation. If the item is considered 50 percent depreciated, you'd receive $1,000.

Question 140: **What is a deductible?**

The deductible is the amount you agree to pay out of your pocket before the insurance company covers the rest of your loss. The higher the deductible, the less expensive the insurance. When choosing a deductible, you're deciding how much risk you're willing to take and balancing risk and cost. Most property deductibles are between $250 and $500 per year.

Question 141: **How might moving to a new city affect what I pay for car insurance?**

Auto insurance costs can vary dramatically from one city to the next. Obviously you'd expect rates to be higher in large cities, but the size of the city is not the only thing that determines rates. If you're moving to a new city, call an insurance agent there (you can find agents on the Internet) and get a quote on coverage for the make and model of your vehicle so you don't have any unpleasant surprises when you arrive.

Chapter 11

BUYING A HOME

BUYING A HOME is the most expensive decision you'll ever make. It's also an emotional and stressful experience for most people, combining excitement, anxiety, fear, and joy. There's a lot of information you have to absorb to make wise house buying and financing decisions, from deciding if owning is really for you, to understanding the nuances of home mortgages.

You'd like to have the American Dream—owning your own home—but you're not sure if you can swing it financially. How much will you have to come up with for a down payment and closing costs? How do you know how high a mortgage you'll qualify for, how much you can really afford based on your lifestyle (regardless of whether the bank thinks you can afford more or less than that), and how much you'll save in taxes?

Maybe you're not sure if you really want to buy a house. Home ownership isn't for everyone, and that's okay. If you change jobs often or get transferred every few years, it may not make sense to buy right now. It usually takes at least five years to recoup the money you pay in up-front costs and the cost of selling.

Question 142: What should I do before I start house hunting?

Before you start house hunting, there are some things you should do that will make the entire process easier. Establish a record of paying your bills on time. Avoid taking out any new loans or applying for any new credit cards in the months before you start looking for a house. Pay off as much debt as possible to help you qualify for the loan and to give you more expendable income after you move in.

Check your credit report. It's the first thing a lender will do when you apply for prequalification or a mortgage, so it's a good idea for you to do it first. Make sure there's nothing in it that's inaccurate or will raise a potential lender's eyebrow. Be prepared to explain any late or missed payments.

Question 143: Why do I need a down payment?

A down payment is the amount of money you pay upfront when you buy property, and it reduces the amount of money you need to borrow. The larger the down payment, the smaller your loan and monthly payments will be, but it's difficult to save enough for a sizeable down payment and closing costs that require cash (real-estate transfer taxes, escrows for property taxes and insurance, title insurance, attorney's fees, loan origination fees, and so on).

There are several options for coming up with more cash. One is to go on a crash budget for a few months by cutting your spending to the bare minimum and saving as much cash as possible. While you wouldn't want to stick to a budget this strict for long, you may be able to do it for a few months. Another method is to sock away all the extra money that comes your way: income tax refunds, overtime, bonuses, cash gifts, or—if you're lucky—lottery winnings. You may have a relative who's willing to lend you money, but it's not legal to borrow money for your down payment unless you identify the loan as a debt and can still qualify. Otherwise your lender will require a statement that the money is a gift.

Question 144: **How does a mortgage work?**

A mortgage is a legal contract that describes the terms of the loan obtained to buy a piece of property. It stipulates that if you don't meet the repayment terms of the loan, the lender can take your property and sell it to get his money back. This process is known as foreclosure.

Mortgage payments are divided between principal (the amount you borrowed) and interest (the cost of borrowing the money). Each month a little bit more gets applied to the principal balance (very little!). On a traditional thirty-year mortgage, the payments for the first twenty years or so will be more interest than principal. For example, on a thirty-year $100,000 mortgage at 7 percent interest, your payments the first year would total $7,983, of which $6,968 would be for interest and only $1,015 for principal. At the end of the year you would still owe a balance of

$98,985. Over the life of the thirty-year mortgage, you'd repay the $100,000 you borrowed plus $139,509 in interest, for a total of $239,509.

Question 145: **Do I need to get private mortgage insurance?**

If it weren't for private mortgage insurance (PMI), which protects the lender in case you're unable to make the payments on your loan, you might not be able to buy a house for many years. Most lenders require a 20 percent down payment, so on a $100,000 loan, you'd be required to come up with approximately $25,000 for the down payment and closing costs. PMI, which ranges between $40 and $100 per month, helps you buy a house with as little as 5 to 10 percent down and is folded into your loan payments.

Under federal law, your lender is required to automatically terminate PMI when your equity reaches 22 percent of the original appraised value of your home. To calculate what percent equity you have in your home, divide your loan balance by the appraised value and deduct this number from 100.

If you bought your home after 1999, your lender must terminate your PMI when you reach 20 percent equity, if you request it. Some businesses offer a service to help you get your PMI dropped, but don't waste your money. Just call your lender and ask if you're paying PMI and if so, when it can be canceled. Then be sure to call again when that time arrives. If you have an FHA or VA loan, PMI isn't required because the federal government has already agreed to protect the lender if you default on your loan.

Question 146: **How do mortgage terms differ?**

Most mortgages are for fifteen, twenty, or thirty years with an interest rate that's fixed over the life of the loan. Payments on fifteen- and twenty-year loans are somewhat higher than those on traditional thirty-year loans, so it requires higher income to qualify for the shorter terms. The benefit is that you build equity faster, pay your mortgage off years sooner, and save many tens of thousands of dollars.

To illustrate the difference between a thirty-year and a fifteen-year mortgage, take the example of a mortgage for $150,000 at 6 percent. The payment on a fifteen-year loan would be $1,266 per month, and the total interest paid over the life of the loan would be $77,841. The payment on a thirty-year mortgage for the same amount and the same interest rate would be $899 per month (a decrease of $367) and the total interest paid over the life of the loan would be $173,757 (an increase of $95,916). Moreover, interest rates on shorter-term mortgages are generally lower than those on longer-term mortgages, so the difference between the two loans in the example would actually be even greater.

Question 147: **What is an adjustable-rate mortgage?**

The interest rates on adjustable-rate mortgages (ARMs) vary. They often start out as much as 1.5 to 2 percentage points lower than the prevailing market rates and increase or decrease at predetermined intervals. The rate is fixed for a certain period (between six months and five years) and then adjusted periodically, like every year or two. The amount the rate can increase at each interval is usually 2 percentage points, and there's often a lifetime cap of 6 percentage points.

Question 148: **Should I choose an ARM over a traditional mortgage?**

In a time of rising interest rates, it can be disturbing to know that your rate can increase every year. Before taking out an ARM, be sure that you can afford the highest payment possible under the terms of the loan. ARMs might be a good option if you know you'll only be in the house for a few years, but if you use one because you can't qualify for a conventional mortgage, you're risking the possible loss of your house.

Question 149: **How does a balloon mortgage work?**

Balloon mortgages have lower interest rates than traditional mortgages, but the loan term is only for five to seven years. At the end of that time, the entire balance is due, and you have to either pay it off or refinance at the rates that are in effect then. If you plan to sell your house, pay it off, or refinance it within the time frame of the loan, this might be an option for you.

Question 150: **What are "points"?**

Points are a percentage of the loan amount that you pay upfront to "buy down" the interest rate on a mortgage. One point is 1 percent of the loan and usually lowers the interest rate by ¼ percent. One point on a $100,000 loan would be $1,000, two points would be $2,000, and so on. When comparing interest rates, you have to consider points. A 7 percent loan with one point is not necessarily better (or worse) than an 8 percent loan with no points. Remember, you have to look at the APR to compare rates and fees. Paying points in order to get a lower interest rate may be worthwhile if you're planning to stay in the house for five years or more. The lower interest rate saves you a lot of money over the long-term, but if you sell in less than five to ten years you won't have time to recoup your costs.

Question 151: **How can I determine the size of the mortgage I will need?**

To estimate how much you can expect to borrow, use the two basic guidelines that banks and mortgage companies follow. The first guideline is that principal, interest, taxes, and insurance (PITI) shouldn't exceed 28 percent of your gross income (your pay before taxes). The second guideline is that PITI plus all your other long-term debt shouldn't exceed 36 percent of your gross income (your long-term debt shouldn't exceed 8 percent of your income). If you make a small down payment, your lender may only use the lower percentages for PITI and long-term debt to protect itself against the possibility that you might default on your loan. However, there's a growing trend for lenders to automatically use the 28 percent guideline for PITI.

Question 152: **What's the difference between being "pre-approved" and being "prequalified" for a mortgage?**

Prequalification means the lender has looked at your credit report, income, and level of debt and determined that you appear to qualify for a loan. Preapproval means that the lender has actually approved you for a specific loan amount. Preapproval gives you the most credibility with the seller, who may be deciding between two or more offers and doesn't want to accept an offer from someone who may not qualify for the financing.

Mortgage brokers bring lenders and borrowers together but do not lend money or service loans. Their fee is added to the cost of your loan. If you don't have great credit, you may get a better rate through a broker than through a bank, but watch out for the fees.

Question 153: **How do I go about making an offer on the house I want?**

Once you've found the house you want to buy, the next step is to make an offer, which is a legally binding contract. The offer will be in writing and will include the amount you're willing to pay for the house (it can be more or less than the asking price) and the time frame for the purchase. It will be contingent on a satisfactory house inspection and bank approval. You'll pay earnest money, usually $1,000, which will be credited to the sales price if the sale goes through. In most cases (but not always), you'll get your money back even if the deal falls through. Fees may be deducted, and the seller and buyer usually have to come to an agreement about how to handle the balance.

Question 154: **What happens after I've made an offer?**

The sellers may accept or decline your offer or they may make a counteroffer. Sometimes this takes hours, sometimes days. If you come to an agreement, the buyer will accept your final written offer and the home inspections will take place as quickly as possible. Once you notify your mortgage company that your offer has been accepted, they'll perform an appraisal to make sure the house is worth what you offered. When all is in place, you and the seller will sign the Purchase and Sale Agreement.

Question 155: **The seller has accepted my offer. Now what?**

After your bank gives the final approval for your loan, and you have proof of homeowner's insurance on the property, you'll be ready to close the deal. Just prior to the closing, you'll walk through the house, which should be empty and clean, and make sure there are no surprises. Then you'll meet with the seller or his representative, the closing attorney, and your Realtor to sign the mortgage papers and make the transfer of the property. Don't be surprised if you feel both excited and nervous. Buying a home is exciting but it's also a big financial commitment.

Question 156: **What are closing costs?**

Closing costs are all of the costs associated with the transfer of the property, the processing of your mortgage, and the fees charged by those who make it all happen. Closing costs include:

- Attorney's fees
- Property transfer fees charged by state and local governments
- Property taxes and homeowner's insurance placed in an escrow account (so that they're available to pay when due)
- Real-estate commissions
- Lender fees such as appraisal, processing fees, points, origination fees, land surveys, interest from the settlement date until your first payment is due, and title insurance

Closing costs vary by location but are typically 3 to 6 percent of your loan, so if you're buying a $100,000 house, you can expect closing costs to be between $3,000 and $6,000. Like the down payment, closing costs must be paid at the time of purchase. Federal law requires lenders to provide you with a Good Faith Estimate of your closing costs before you go to settlement.

Chapter 12

GETTING MARRIED

YOU'RE GETTING MARRIED, and there are decisions to make about merging your finances. Later, you may find yourself planning for a baby, deciding if you can afford to be a stay-at-home parent, and trying to raise financially savvy kids. And although you probably don't want to consider the possibility, you may need to know how to protect yourself if your marriage ends in divorce.

For your marriage to succeed you have to agree about the role money will play in your marriage. Open communication about money is key. Once you've decided to tie the knot, discussions about money shouldn't be far behind. When you get married, you take on not only all your loved one's emotional baggage, but all their financial baggage as well. You need to know just how heavy that baggage is.

Question 157: **How can I start talking to my spouse about money matters?**

Some people are very uncomfortable talking about money, so you may want to start out gradually by discussing how your parents handled money and how you feel about its role in your life. For some people, money symbolizes love or security; for others, it symbolizes power or control. It can be something to be spent freely with no thought for tomorrow, or hoarded and saved for the future. Explore your feelings about money together.

Once you're married, your partner's finances will be your finances, for better or for worse. After you've had a few initial discussions about money in general, initiate a discussion about your respective financial situations. Get copies of your credit reports and go over them together. If your fiancé won't talk about money, consider counseling. How can you work toward common goals if one of you can't or won't talk about money?

Question 158: **Should we share a joint account for all our income and paying all our bills?**

It's very difficult to keep track of the transactions that two people make to a single bank account and this can lead to bounced checks and frequent arguments. Many couples find that a joint account for household expenses and individual accounts for each spouse's personal spending works very well. It allows each of you to have discretionary money for expenditures that you don't have to explain or justify to each other.

If one person in a relationship controls the other's spending, it gives the controlling person a parental type of power that's not healthy in a marriage, and can cause resentment to build in the spouse who has no financial power in the relationship.

Question 159: **How should we divide the money-managing responsibilities?**

Often there's one person in a marriage who is more interested, motivated, or adept at paying the bills, balancing the checkbooks, tracking expenses and investments, and maintaining a budget. Talk about it. The person who handles the money should be detail-oriented. You may both quickly agree on the obvious choice for these tasks or you may decide to share the responsibility. Regardless of who does what, sit down at least once a month and review your finances together. What progress have you made toward your joint budgeting and savings goals? Are there any cash shortfalls or large expenditures looming? How are your investments performing?

Question 160: **Do we need a prenuptial agreement?**

Prenuptial agreements may have a negative connotation, but nearly everybody could benefit from one. These agreements designate how your assets and liabilities will be handled in the event of a divorce, but can also be used to protect the interests of children from a previous marriage or spell out other important issues. If you plan to have children of your own, your agreement may contain arrangements for child support, education, or even religious upbringing.

For a prenuptial agreement to be legally binding, each of you has to be represented by your own independent lawyer and must fully disclose all of your assets and liabilities. Prenuptial agreements shouldn't be viewed as planning for a marriage to fail or in any other negative light. They're just good common sense and can save a lot of headaches and heartaches later.

Question 161: **How can we save money on our wedding?**

First of all, draw up a budget. Make a list of everything you can think of that you'll need for the ceremony, rehearsal dinner, and reception and your estimate of what each item will cost. Refine your budget as you get price quotes, and identify the things that are most important to you. Small compromises can often add up to big savings.

The biggest factor influencing your costs is the number of guests that attend. If your average cost per person for food, drink, linens, cutlery, china, and other things you have to rent by the person is $50, knocking twenty people off your guest list will save you $1,000 plus tips. Inviting just the people who really matter can save you thousands of dollars.

Question 162: **What is the "marriage tax penalty"?**

The standard deduction you're allowed to take from your taxable income when you're married filing jointly is less than the amount the two of you could deduct when you were single. The standard deduction for 2002 was $4,700, so if you were still single, the standard deduction would total $9,400 for the two of you. It's only $7,850 for a married couple filing jointly—$1,550 less than you could deduct between you when you were single.

The problem doesn't stop there. The 15 percent tax bracket for singles ends at $27,950 of taxable income; so two single people would be taxed at 15 percent up to a combined total of $55,900. The 15 percent tax bracket for married couples filing jointly ends at $46,700, a difference of $9,200 ($55,900 − $46,700). As a married couple you'd pay 27 percent instead of 15 percent, for a total additional tax bite of $1,104 ($9,200 times the additional

12 percent difference between the 15 percent bracket and the 27 percent bracket).

Question 163: **How can we avoid a big tax bill in April?**

If you both checked "married" on your new W-4 at work, your payroll departments will calculate withholding based on the standard deduction of $7,850 for married individuals. Your taxes will be withheld as though you were entitled to twice the standard deduction and thus will be significantly underwithheld. To prevent this from happening, after you get married you should file new W-4s with your respective employers with one of you checking the married status and the other checking the single status.

Question 164: **How can my new spouse and I start to combine our finances?**

Go through the documentation for your retirement plans, life insurance policies, bank accounts, and investment accounts. If you want your spouse to be the beneficiary, file change of beneficiary forms. Also look for accounts you want to add your spouse's name to as joint owner, or where you need to change the name of the person to notify in an emergency. If one of you owns property, decide whether you want to change the deed to include both your names.

Question 165: **What do I need to do if I'm changing my name?**

Make sure to apply for a new Social Security card, vehicle title, and driver's license in your new name. Have a will drawn up, or if you already have one, have it updated or rewritten. Notify banks, insurance companies, brokerages, and others about your name change. Be aware that if you add your name to your spouse's existing credit card, you'll be equally responsible for the debt that he or she brought in to the marriage.

Have a will drawn up, or if you already have one, have it updated or rewritten. If one of you has children from a previous relationship, it's especially important to spell out guardianship and custody issues.

Question 166: **We are thinking about starting a family soon. How do we start planning for a new arrival?**

As soon as you have your first thought about having a baby, start a baby fund to cover unexpected costs, and contribute to it monthly. Shop for bargains on baby equipment and supplies, but don't skimp on items that affect safety, like high-quality car seats. Don't go over-board on toys and baby accessories that will be quickly outgrown and that the baby is too young to appreciate. These add up to big bucks.

Think about how you'll manage on one income during mater-nity leave and possibly reduced income during the pregnancy. Are you covered by short-term disability insurance? If so, you'll receive between 60 percent and 70 percent of your regular income for approximately six weeks following delivery, or sooner if you're deemed medically unable to work during your pregnancy.

Question 167: **How do we handle our new family's health insurance needs?**

The most immediate issue when you're thinking of adding a new member to your family is health insurance. Estimate how much you can expect to pay out of your own pocket, based on the cov-erage provided by your health insurance policy. If you're covered under an HMO, you'll probably have a copay for each doctor visit (usually $10 to $25) and a copay for the hospital admission for the delivery (usually a minimum of $250 to $500). Check your policy to see what other costs you might incur. Be sure your doctor and the hospital are in your HMO network or you could be faced with some very large medical bills.

Find out how much it will cost to add your new family member to your group medical insurance policy as a dependent. If you and your spouse have separate insurance policies, figure out if it makes sense for one of you to transfer to the other's policy. Dependent coverage may be cheaper if you're all on one policy, especially if one spouse has a cafeteria (section 125) plan and pays premiums with pretax dollars.

Question 168: **When should I start teaching my children about money?**

You can start teaching your kids about the basics of spending, banking, and saving when they are around the age of five. Let them make their own bank deposits and withdrawals, make purchases, and decide what to spend their money on (within reason). Give advice, but don't control. It's important for them to be allowed to make mistakes so they can learn about consequences and choices.

Kids should receive an allowance by the time they're in school. The purpose of the allowance is to teach them about managing money. Help them decide how much of each week's allowance they'll put in the bank. They'll quickly learn that if they spend it now, they won't have it when something they really want comes along. An allowance helps them learn to save and to prioritize. Teach your kids with practical everyday examples when the opportunities arise. Real life examples will sink in much more readily than abstract lectures with no immediate practical application.

Question 169: **If my spouse and I get divorced, how can I protect myself financially?**

If you and your spouse agree to a division of your debt, be sure to make this a formal arrangement by contacting each creditor and asking them to legally transfer the debt to you or your spouse and release the other from liability. If you're going to be responsible for a debt, your spouse's name shouldn't be listed as an authorized user (for example, on a credit card) and he or she shouldn't be held responsible if you fail to pay it off—and vice versa.

Some couples obtain individual consolidation loans and pay off their portion of the joint debts so the accounts can be closed. This is ideal for a clean split, but if it's not possible and your spouse incurs large amounts of debt, inform the lender in writing that you're no longer responsible for any new charges.

Question 170: **How can I protect my children in the event of a divorce?**

If your marriage is headed for divorce and you're the custodial parent, file for child support as soon as you and your spouse separate. Your spouse has no legal obligation to pay child support unless there's a court order from a divorce, marriage dissolution, establishment of paternity, or legal separation. An attorney or your local child support agency can help you get a court order. Child support judgments are issued as of the date of filing and are not retroactive.

If you're not the custodial parent, remember that you can break the bond of marriage but you can never break the bond of parenthood. Your responsibility to your children continues even after your marriage ends. Child support payments should be one of your highest financial priorities.

Chapter 13

STAYING SINGLE

MILLIONS OF COUPLES live together without the benefits of marriage, many unaware of the legal and financial consequences of their arrangement. If you're living with your partner, you should consider the issues involved with mingling your assets and sharing your expenses and take steps to protect yourself in case your relationship ends.

Whether you're getting married or just moving in together, it's a good time to talk about your finances. Inform your partner of any skeletons in your financial closet, such as bad credit, a past bankruptcy, a lien on your house, unpaid child support, or a tax lien. Since you'll be mingling finances to some extent, it's only fair to be upfront about these things and start your time together on the right foot. It's likely your partner will find out about any financial issues once you're living together anyway, and may feel that your failure to share this information earlier reflects badly on your relationship. You can always change the way you do things after you've lived together for a while, but don't wait until then to discuss how you're going to handle the money issues that affect you both, from spending habits to investments and financial goals.

Question 171: **Why do we even need a nonmarital agreement?**

The best legal protection for unmarried couples living together is a nonmarital agreement, also referred to as a cohabitation, relationship, or "living together" agreement. It's a written contract that gives each of you legal control over your property and finances if the relationship ends, and it can save you attorney's fees and court costs if there's any disagreement about who gets what.

Remember that 50 percent of marriages end in divorce, and an even larger percentage of unwed couples eventually go their separate ways. If you're in your twenties and haven't accumulated many assets yet, a nonmarital agreement may seem totally unnecessary. If your relationship is likely to be short-term, you may be right. But if you're in a committed relationship that you expect to be long-term, a nonmarital agreement is important.

Question 172: **What is included in a nonmarital agreement?**

Nonmarital agreements can cover a wide range of issues but are especially critical if you're buying a house together, purchasing other large assets with joint funds, coming into the relationship with previously owned property or assets, or if one of you has a lot of debt. If your partner has large debts, you should protect yourself against creditors who may seize joint property if your partner falls behind in the payments.

It's a good idea to include a clause stating that mediation will be used for resolving any disputes and that if you still can't come to an agreement after mediation you'll go to formal and binding arbitration. This will save you from the expense and hassle of a messy lawsuit.

Question 173: **How is common-law marriage defined?**

In a common-law marriage, you're considered married even though you've never gone through the formalities. The number of years it takes before you're considered married by common law is not clearly defined in any of the twelve states that recognize common-law marriages. There's also no simple way to determine if you're married by common law, and it usually only comes up if you have to go to court for a legal matter related to your relationship.

There's a common misperception that if you live together for seven years you're married by common law. No states specify a minimum number of years. The states that recognize common-law marriages fully are Alabama, Colorado, Iowa, Kansas, Montana, Oklahoma, Pennsylvania, Rhode Island, South Carolina, Texas, Utah, and Washington, D.C.

Question 174: **If we're not planning to get married, why do we need to discuss our finances?**

If it's important to discuss the mingling of your assets and finances when you're planning to get married, it's even more important if you're moving in together without the legal benefits of marriage. If either or both of you own assets that you'll be sharing it's especially critical. Even if you don't think it's necessary when you first move in together, if you find that you're accumulating joint property, consider clarifying who owns what in a legal document.

Question 175: **What is a joint purchase agreement?**

Some couples use a joint purchase agreement when they buy large items together, if they don't have a nonmarital contract that covers how these purchases will be handled. Joint purchase agreements spell out what will happen to an item purchased with joint funds if the relationship ends for any reason, without addressing the broader issues usually included in a nonmarital agreement.

If you don't have a written agreement about how assets purchased together will be dealt with if your relationship ends, you should document your contribution for these assets. When you buy an asset together, get a receipt as evidence that you contributed toward ownership of the asset. Better yet, pay your portion by check and make a notation on the check itself, such as "50 percent of the jointly owned bedroom furniture."

Question 176: **How can we protect our rights if we want to buy a house together?**

The simplest method of transferring property is joint ownership with rights of survivorship, which means that if one of you dies, the other automatically inherits the property. You avoid inheritance tax because the house isn't considered part of the estate. The downside is that you don't have the option of selling your share or leaving it to someone other than your partner, and joint ownership provisions in the deed will override any bequest in your will.

Tenants in common means that each of you owns half of the house. If you die, your share will go to the person or persons indicated in your will (if you have one), or else to your next of kin. This method of ownership allows for owners with unequal equity. For example, you may own 75 percent of the house and your partner may own 25 percent. Each of you can sell or give away your share or leave it to one or more individuals of your choice, such as kids from a previous relationship. Having a will is critical if you own property as tenants in common.

Question 177: **How do we decide who gets the house if we break up?**

Your nonmarital agreement should spell out what will happen if both of you want to keep the house when you break up. How will you decide who goes and who stays? Does the person who gets the house buy out the person who's leaving? How is the buy-out price calculated? Is it half the equity in the house, or is an amount deducted equal to the Realtor fees that would have been paid if the house had been sold?

If one of you contributed more to the purchase of the house than the other, your nonmarital agreement should spell out how this will be compensated if you break up. Even if you each contributed 50 percent, you may want to allow for one person to build equity or offset contributions to the household fund by doing repairs or improvements on the house.

Question 178: **How should we divide household expenses if one of us earns significantly more than the other?**

Although many of the issues faced by unmarried couples living together are very different from those that married couples face, the issues surrounding the sharing of expenses is common to both.

While the actual method you decide on for sharing expenses may be unimportant, to avoid disagreements later you should discuss upfront how you want to handle this issue. Will you divide housing costs and day-to-day expenses equally or contribute to a household fund in proportion to your income? The latter may be the fairest method if one of you earns significantly more than the other. For example, let's say one of you makes $40,000 per year and the other makes $20,000. The one that makes twice as much will contribute $2 for every $1 the other contributes to the joint household fund.

Question 179: **Is it best to keep one joint or two separate bank accounts?**

If you choose to maintain separate accounts, it's a good idea to document your intention to share expenses by paying your portion of bills directly rather than paying your partner your share in cash or by check. This documents the implied contract (mentioned previously) and could protect you if your relationship ends in court. If you decide to have a joint bank account, be aware that either of you could legally take all the money out of the account. Many people have ended a live-in relationship by walking away with the cash and leaving their partner high and dry. It's safer to keep separate bank accounts, especially in the early years of your relationship.

Question 180: **If we own a house together, how do we decide who gets to take the mortgage deduction?**

When you own a house together, the issue of who will get to claim the mortgage interest and property tax deductions for federal income tax return purposes has to be addressed. You could split the deductions in half, but you might not benefit as much from this method if one of you makes significantly more than the other, because the deductions will create more tax savings for the person with the higher tax rate. It might make more sense to let that person claim the entire deduction and compensate the other person in some monetary way.

Question 181: **Can one of us claim "head of household" status on our tax return even though we're not married?**

If a dependent child lives with you and your unmarried partner at least six months a year, and you provide more than 50 percent of the cost of maintaining the household, you can claim head of household status on your income tax return. This allows you to take the child and dependent care credits to reduce your taxes. See IRS Publication 17, Chapter 33, for detailed information on the "head of household" status and a checklist to see if you're qualified to claim it.

If your income is below the limit, you can also take the earned income tax credit, which offsets your income tax liability and can sometimes supplement your income by allowing you to get back more than you actually paid. If you have a dependent child living with you, you may want to consult a tax accountant before filing your income tax returns.

Question 182: **Why do I need a will?**

Dying intestate means dying without a written will. Each state has laws that designate the method of distributing your property if you die intestate, and there's a good chance your property won't go to the individuals you'd want to receive it. If you have kids, it's absolutely critical, because your will is the instrument for indicating who you'd want to take guardianship, something that is much too important to leave to chance or the courts.

If you're married, in most states your spouse and children automatically inherit your property if you die intestate. If you're unmarried and die intestate, your property will be divided among your parents, sisters and brothers, and other relatives. Your partner will not receive anything. Without a written nonmarital contract the only way to leave property to your partner if you die is through a will. If you have neither a contract nor a will, the chances of your partner getting anything are slim.

Question 183: **What is an advance directive?**

Dying is not something you usually think much about in your twenties and thirties, but it happens to people of all ages, so think about taking steps to protect your loved one, especially if he or she develops a serious illness.

An advance directive is a legal document identifying the treatments and lifesaving measures you want if you become ill and there's no reasonable hope of recovery. There are two basic types of advance directives: a living will and a durable power of attorney for health care. In a living will, you state the kind of health care you want under certain circumstances and the kind you don't want. For example, if you're terminally ill, you may not want to be resuscitated if you stop breathing. In a durable power of attorney for health care, also called a health care proxy, you designate somebody close to you to make decisions about your health care if you're unable to make them for yourself.

It's a good idea to have both types of advance directives. If you want your partner to be the person making health care decisions for you if you're unable to, a durable power of attorney for health care is a must.

PART **IV**

Planning for Tomorrow

Chapter 14

INSURING YOUR FUTURE

THE PURPOSE OF insurance is to protect your assets against catastrophic losses that could damage your financial future. Whether that asset is a house, a car, or your income-earning ability, insurance protects you from financial disaster. Decide how much risk you can assume and insure the rest.

If you finance a new car or other large purchase, you'll probably be offered credit life insurance. Do you need it? Probably not. What about contact lens insurance? Air travel insurance? Rental car insurance? No, no, and probably not. Your personal auto insurance usually covers you for rental cars, but call your insurance agent to find out for sure.

Question 184: **Do I need life insurance?**

You may or may not need life insurance, depending on your personal situation. If you don't need it, don't buy it. It may give you a false sense of security but you'll be wasting your money. To figure out whether or not you need life insurance, consider its purpose, which is to replace income in the event of the policyholder's death. If you're single and have no dependents, nobody is relying on the income you bring in, so you don't need life insurance.

If you're a stay-at-home parent and aren't making a significant contribution to the household income, you probably don't need life insurance. The money could best be invested or used elsewhere. On the other hand, if your salary is important to supporting your family, paying the mortgage, or sending your kids to college, life insurance can ensure that these financial obligations are covered in the event of your death.

Question 185: **How much does life insurance cost?**

The cost of pure life insurance is based on actuarial tables that project your life expectancy. If you're considered a high risk—for instance if you're overweight or a smoker, have a pre-existing health condition, or a dangerous hobby or occupation (flying, for example)—you'll pay higher rates. It's not a good idea to lie about any of these factors on your application. The insurance company could end up refusing to pay your beneficiaries if they find that you didn't tell the truth.

Question 186: **I'm young and healthy—do I really need health insurance?**

No matter how old (or young) you are, you need health insurance to protect yourself against financial disaster if you become seriously ill or have an accident. These things happen to people of all ages. It's extremely foolhardy to go without some type of health insurance at any age. If you simply can't afford the premiums, buy a policy with a very high deductible ($5,000 for example) to limit your exposure.

If you have health insurance, you're most likely covered under a group plan provided by your employer or your spouse's employer. Some people who don't have the benefit of a group plan through work purchase their own individual policies or are covered under COBRA (more on that a little later). Others have no coverage at all.

Question 187: **What is an HMO?**

A Health Maintenance Organization (HMO) is an association of health care professionals and medical facilities that sell a fixed package of health care services for a fixed price. Each patient has a primary-care physician, who is often referred to as a gatekeeper because services provided by a specialist are not covered unless the gatekeeper determines that the specialist is necessary.

The advantages of HMOs are lower and more predictable out-of-pocket costs and no claim forms. The major disadvantage is that services provided by health care professionals outside the network of your HMO aren't covered. If your network is small, your choices of doctors and other health professionals will be very limited, and services provided by specialists will be dependent on a referral from your primary physician. In HMOs, it's possible that you might not receive the medical care you need due to incentives paid to HMO doctors by the insurance company that reward doctors who limit tests and referrals to specialists.

Question 188: **What's the difference between an HMO and a PPO?**

Preferred Provider Organizations (PPOs) combine the managed care aspects of an HMO with the flexibility of a fee-for-service plan. When you use doctors in your approved network, more of your medical costs are covered, but you can go outside the network of health care professionals and facilities to any health care provider of your choice when you feel it's necessary. The main advantage of a PPO is the flexibility and a wide choice of doctors and facilities. The only disadvantage is that it's more difficult to predict your out-of-pocket costs and you'll pay more for your health care if you go out of network.

Question 189: **What is COBRA?**

Under the Consolidated Omnibus Reconciliation Act (COBRA) of 1986, employees who lose medical and dental insurance for certain reasons can often buy group coverage for themselves and their dependents for a specified period of time at group rates. The law applies to group health plans maintained by private sector and state and local government employers with twenty or more full- and part-time employees in the prior year. It doesn't apply to plans maintained by the federal government or church organizations.

Question 190: **How can I use my COBRA coverage?**

It's your responsibility to notify your employer or your spouse's employer within sixty days of a qualifying event that the plan administrator might not know about, such as legal separation, divorce, or a child reaching the maximum age to be a covered dependent. Once you elect coverage, you're required to pay premiums retroactive to the date of the qualifying event, which will provide you with continuous health insurance with no lapse in coverage. Your cost for COBRA coverage is the employer's actual cost plus a 2 percent administrative fee. You have the same grace period that the employer is given by the insurance company, usually thirty days. If you don't pay the premium within the grace period, your coverage will be terminated. Each qualified beneficiary may elect COBRA coverage independently of any other qualified beneficiary.

Question 191: **Why would I need disability insurance?**

Ironically, although the likelihood of becoming disabled is greater than the likelihood of dying during any given period of time, more people buy life insurance than disability insurance. Your greatest asset is your ability to generate income. Shouldn't you insure it? You're never too young or healthy to require disability insurance. While it's true that your chances of experiencing a period of disability are greater as you get older, illness and accidents can happen to you at any age. You could suffer a sports injury, a back injury, or an injury caused by a car accident. You could come down with mono and be out of commission for a few weeks or months.

Before purchasing an individual disability policy, be sure you understand the terms used and read the policy carefully to make sure you know what benefits you're getting. Find out if there are any exclusions, what the elimination period is, what the benefit period is, and the definition of total disability.

Question 192: **What's the difference between short-term and long-term disability insurance?**

If you become disabled, you'll receive benefits until you recover or reach the maximum benefit provided by your policy. Short-term disability policies pay benefits for a shorter period of time, from six weeks to two years. Long-term disability policies pay benefits for several years or until the age of sixty-five (or longer). The shorter the elimination period and the longer the benefit period, the higher the premium will be.

Question 193: **What is an "elimination period"?**

An elimination period is the period of time after you become unable to work before you can begin receiving benefits under the policy. A short-term disability policy may have an elimination period of one to two weeks for illness or a shorter time for accidents. Long-term disability elimination periods are typically at least thirty days and more commonly ninety days. Most policies replace only 60 percent of your income, up to a maximum of $5,000 to $10,000 per month.

Question 194: **How is "disability" defined for insurance purposes?**

The best policies will have a definition of disability that includes the inability to perform the major duties of your own occupation. Under these policies, if you're unable to perform your major duties, you can go to work in a different occupation that you are able to perform and still collect your disability pay. Less expensive or lower-quality policies won't pay benefits unless you're unable to do virtually any work, or they'll offset your monthly benefit check against any income you're earning elsewhere.

Question 195: **Why do I need homeowner's insurance?**

Homeowner's insurance protects you if your home and any structures attached to it or other structures on your property are damaged or destroyed. It also covers your home's contents if they're damaged or destroyed, and it helps protect you from liability and medical costs if someone is hurt on your property. If you own a home you can't afford to be without this coverage. If you want to keep costs down, choose a higher deductible, but don't forgo the insurance altogether.

Question 196: **What types of homeowner's insurance are there?**

There are several basic types of homeowner's policies. They vary by the types of perils, or potential damages, covered and by the extent of coverage. For example, some policies reimburse you only for the depreciated value of your belongings. You'd have to pay out of pocket to replace the items that were destroyed. Replacement coverage, on the other hand, reimburses you for the cost to replace those items at their current prices. You should always choose replacement coverage.

If you had to file a claim under your homeowner's insurance, think about how you'd prove what you lost in a fire or other damage to your home. You'd never be able to remember every item you owned. It's a good idea to take an inventory of your household belongings by going through every room and writing down each item, and to the best of your memory, when you bought it, where you bought it, and how much you paid for it. Photos are helpful for expensive or unique items. Some people use a video camera to take their inventory. Regardless of how you do it, keep a copy of the inventory someplace other than in your home so you'd have access to it if your home were damaged.

Question 197: **What is covered by auto insurance?**

Most states require you to have bodily injury liability insurance on your vehicle, which pays your medical bills and lost wages, the medical bills of others hurt in an accident you caused, and property damage, up to the limits you've chosen. The limits are shown in thousands of dollars as bodily injury for one person/bodily injury for more than one person/property damage. Personal injury protection or medical coverage pays your own medical costs if you're injured in an accident. It's required in approximately one-third of all states. Some states also require you to buy additional coverage that will cover your medical costs and lost wages if you're injured in an accident caused by an uninsured motorist.

The legally required minimums for liability coverage are so low that they're not adequate if you own a house or other assets that an injured person could come after if your insurance wasn't enough to cover his or her medical expenses. Unless you have no assets to speak of, you should elect limits of at least 100/300 for bodily injury.

Chapter 15

PAYING TAXES

FILLING OUT THE forms properly is not even half the battle when it comes to taxes. You also want to avoid penalties and keep as much of your money as possible by taking advantage of every tax-saving strategy available to you. That requires a basic understanding of how taxes work and an awareness of significant tax-reduction opportunities.

Most people have too much tax withheld and let the IRS borrow their money interest-free all year. You could be earning interest on that money or saving between 12 and 20 percent in interest charges by using the extra money to pay down credit card debt. The only time it makes sense to have more withheld than you're going to owe is if you find it impossible to save money on a regular basis. You could accomplish the same thing by having a fixed amount automatically deducted from your check each month and deposited in a savings account.

Question 198: **How do tax exemptions work?**

An exemption is a fixed amount you deduct from your taxable income for yourself, your spouse if you're married, and each eligible dependent you claim on your income tax return. In 2002, each exemption was worth $3,000, so if you're married but have no kids, you can claim $6,000 if you file jointly. The exemption phases out at certain income levels but unless you're single with income over $137,300 or married with combined income over $206,000, you'll be able to take the full deduction.

Question 199: **How can I determine my "effective tax rate"?**

Your effective tax rate is the tax rate you actually pay on your total income, considering that part of your income isn't taxed at all due to exemptions and the standard deduction or itemized deductions, and part of your income may fall in different tax brackets. To calculate your effective federal tax rate, divide your total federal income taxes for the year (from your latest tax return) by your total income.

Question 200: **What is the difference between itemized and standard deductions?**

A standard deduction is a fixed dollar amount that you deduct from your taxable income. If your allowable itemized deductions total more than the standard deduction, you'll save money by itemizing. To see if you qualify, use a copy of Schedule A from Form 1040 to list the amounts of each of the deductions that apply to you, such as home mortgage interest, real-estate taxes, state income taxes, and personal-property taxes. If the total is more than the standard deduction, itemize.

So many deductions have disappeared over the years that if you have no mortgage interest or very low mortgage interest, you probably won't be able to itemize unless you have extremely large medical expenses or charitable contributions.

Question 201: **I'm not an accountant—can I really file my taxes on my own?**

Just the thought of preparing your own tax return may make you shudder, but the average person is more than capable of completing Form 1040EZ and Form 1040A (the short form). Form 1040 (the long form) is definitely more challenging but is much less so thanks to the availability of robust tax preparation software programs for your personal computer. The biggest requirement is time.

Doing your own taxes is easy using tax software like TurboTax. You can buy the software from office supply stores or download it online. If you don't want to buy new tax software every year, you can use web-based software. The main advantage now to web-based software is that you don't have to be on your own PC to work on your return. You can do so from any computer that has access to the Internet.

Question 202: **If I don't want to handle my taxes myself, how do I find someone I can trust to do it for me?**

Start by asking friends, family, coworkers, and other professionals, like bankers, for recommendations. If you can't come up with a recommendation this way, try contacting the local chapter of a professional association like the American Institute of Certified Public Accountants (AICPA). Once you've identified someone you'd like to use, talk to him or her on the phone and ask about qualifications, background, and fees. Find out whether this person works full-time or part-time doing tax consulting, number of years of experience, and participation in continuing professional education. The latter is important because tax preparers need to keep up with yearly changes in tax laws. When you've made a decision, make an appointment well in advance of the filing deadline. Most tax professionals become totally booked up for the tax season early in the year.

Question 203: **What can I do to reduce my taxes?**

One of the easiest ways to reduce your taxes is to take advantage of tax-free or tax-deferred employer-provided fringe benefits, such as benefits provided under cafeteria plans and flexible spending accounts that allow you to take benefits in lieu of cash (tax-free), medical and accident insurance paid by your employer (tax-free), educational assistance programs (tax-free), retirement plans like 401(k) and 403(b) that allow you to make contributions (tax-deferred), employee stock purchase plans (tax-deferred), and group term health insurance up to $50,000 (tax-free).

Another way to reduce taxes is to be sure you take all the credits and other tax-reductions you're entitled to, such as the child credit (in addition to claiming the child as a dependent), filing as head of household, or taking the earned income tax credit if you qualify.

Question 204: **What types of records do I need to keep?**

Hang on to any documents that identify your sources of income (W-2s, 1099s), help determine the value of assets (brokerage and mutual fund statements), and prove your deductions (receipts or invoices and canceled checks, property tax statements, mortgage interest statements, and proof of any business expenses if you file Schedule C). Checks alone may not prove the deductibility of an expense. The best proof is an itemized invoice accompanied by a canceled check proving that you paid it.

Keep your tax records in a separate file for each year. After six years you can throw the backup documents away if storage space is an issue, but keep your income tax returns, retirement account statements, home purchase or sale documents, and stock or other investment documents indefinitely.

Question 205: **How can I avoid being audited?**

Nobody likes to have the taxman come knocking on the door. There are a few simple steps you can take to reduce your chances of being audited, but if you're one of the 0.5 percent who get chosen randomly for the experience, don't panic. Being prepared is more than half the battle.

The most basic thing you can do to reduce your chances of being audited is to make sure there are no math errors on your return. Too many math errors will red flag your return for review. Make sure Social Security numbers for you and your dependents are accurate. If you won't be able to file your return by the April 15 deadline, file for an extension before the deadline. Attach an explanation for anything that's not obvious. Be sure to sign your return.

Question 206: **How are returns chosen for audit?**

Some steps, such as filing Schedule C for self-employed individuals or claiming the home office deduction, will increase your chances of being audited. But as long as you reported everything accurately and have documentation to prove it, you have nothing to worry about.

The IRS uses something called the discriminant function system (DIF), which assigns a score to key elements on your return. If the total score for your entire return is greater than the IRS guidelines, the computer will kick your return out for review by an IRS agent. If the agent feels your return should be audited after reviewing it, you'll be contacted. A very small percentage of returns are chosen completely by random. There's nothing you can do to reduce your chances except to file close to the filing deadline rather than early. There's some evidence that people who file early may have a greater chance of being randomly selected for audit.

Question 207: **What should I do if I'm being audited?**

During an audit you'll be asked to substantiate certain items by producing receipts or other proof. You may be able to do this by mail. If a face-to-face audit is requested, you have the right to have a representative (your accountant or tax preparer) attend with you or in your place. If you attend, keep your emotions under control, don't volunteer any information, and don't act defensive. Have all of the requested documents with you and well organized. It may be best to let your representative answer all questions or meet with the IRS agent without you. If your representative can't answer a question, he or she will ask you later and get back to the agent. This prevents you from making comments that can get you in hot water and gives you time to think about your answers.

Question 208: **I owe money to the IRS this year, and I cannot afford to pay. What should I do?**

It's a disturbing moment when you finish your tax return and realize you owe additional tax and don't have the money to pay it. Don't panic. First of all, don't compound the problem by filing your tax return late. File by the due date or file for an extension even if you can't pay the tax due. Penalties for late filing can add up to 25 percent to your tax bill. You have a number of options for coming up with the cash later. Try to take out a bank loan for the amount you owe. The interest rate will be lower than the rate charged by the IRS. If that doesn't work, consider using your credit card or applying for a new card with a low introductory rate and paying the balance off before the rate goes up.

Question 209: **How can I make sure I don't owe money next year?**

To ensure that this doesn't happen to you again, review your withholding every year and make sure you're having enough taken out to cover your income. If you receive income that taxes weren't withheld from, make quarterly estimated tax payments or increase the amount of your withholding at work to compensate.

You should change your withholding by filing a new W-4 with your employer to have additional tax taken out each pay period through the end of the year. After the start of the new year, complete another W-4 to adjust your withholding back to a more normal amount. The withholding calculator on the IRS website will help you determine what your withholding should be and is more accurate than the worksheets used on the W-4 form.

Chapter 16

INVESTING WISELY

BEFORE YOU EVEN think about investing, you should have some basics in place. If you have credit card debt, get rid of it before diverting money to investments. Why put your money into an investment with a low or uncertain return when you can immediately earn 15 percent to 20 percent by paying off the balance on your high-interest credit card? If you don't have an emergency fund that would cover three to six months of basic expenses if you lost your job or became unable to work, establish one before tying up your cash in investments. If you're not taking advantage of your employer's 401(k) plan, you're ignoring a great opportunity. You're never too young to start saving for retirement, and a 401(k) is the best way to do it. Not only do you postpone taxes on your earnings, your employer probably matches some portion of your contribution.

Question 210: **Where's the best place to invest my money?**

If you don't need the money for at least five years, the stock market is the best option. You can buy individual stocks and bonds or you can lower your risk by buying mutual funds, which invest in the stocks and bonds of many different companies. The longer the time frame, the more aggressive the investment can be. That's why the bulk of your 401(k) plan or other retirement funds should be in stocks or mutual funds when you're young and won't need the money for several decades. If you're saving for a down payment on a house that you hope to buy in three years, your money should be in much more conservative investments, like CDs and other places to stash your short-term cash.

Question 211: **How do I know how much risk I can tolerate?**

High-risk investors are willing to take major risks in exchange for the possibility of substantial returns. They can still sleep at night even if they lose large amounts of money. Moderate-risk investors are willing to take low to medium risk to increase their chances of investment growth. Conservative investors are uncomfortable at the thought of losing even a small part of their investments and will give up the chance of high returns for the stability and safety of conservative investments with predictable income.

Low-risk investors face a greater risk: not having enough money for retirement. If you don't invest in stocks, you miss out on the most financially rewarding investment. Historically, the stock market has always out-performed other investments over time.

Question 212: **What's the difference between high-risk and low-risk investments?**

The highest-risk investments are futures, commodities, limited partnerships, collectibles, real-estate investment trusts (REITs), penny stocks (stocks that cost under $1 per share), speculative stocks (such as stock in new companies), and high-yield (or "junk") bonds. Moderate-risk investments include growth stocks (companies that reinvest most of their profits to grow the business), corporate bonds with low ratings, balanced mutual funds, aggressive mutual funds, rental real estate, annuities, and international stocks. Limited-risk investments are corporate and municipal bonds with high ratings, index mutual funds, and blue-chip stocks. The lowest-risk investments are Treasury bills, U.S. savings bonds, bank CDs, and money market funds.

Question 213: **What is asset allocation?**

Asset allocation uses a formula to divide your portfolio among the three main types of investments: stocks, bonds, and cash equivalents. An aggressive asset allocation might include 70 percent stocks, 20 percent bonds, and 10 percent cash. A conservative asset allocation might include 40 percent stocks, 40 percent bonds, and 20 percent cash. Because different types of investments grow at different rates, it's a good idea to reallocate your investments once a year. For instance, after you've been investing for a while, you might have a conservative portfolio of 40 percent stocks, 40 percent bonds, and 20 percent cash. If your stocks have a banner year and bonds are sluggish, the value of your portfolio might change to 60 percent stocks, 20 percent bonds, and 20 percent cash. This could cause your portfolio to change from conservative to aggressive without you even realizing it, so you may want to realign it by making some changes in your investments.

Question 214: **How should I distribute my investments?**

Choosing what percentage to invest in each category depends on a number of factors, including your risk tolerance, your age or how much time you have to invest before you need the money, the current state of the market, and what direction interest rates are headed. Most experts recommend that you invest as much as 80 percent of your portfolio in stocks or stock mutual funds if you're in your twenties or thirties.

It's not a good idea to buy bonds when interest rates are expected to rise soon, because you'll be stuck with a lower than market interest rate and will be earning less than you would have if you'd waited a short time.

Question 215: **Why do I need to diversify my assets?**

The more you spread out your investments between different kinds of securities and different sectors of the industry (financial services, biomedical, technology), the lower the risk of substantial losses. A well-diversified portfolio includes cash or cash equivalents (Treasury bills, CDs, etc.), stocks, bonds, and mutual funds. The latter should be divided between small-cap, mid-cap, and large-cap (more on this to follow). Diversifying helps you weather the ups and downs of the market.

Question 216: **What does it mean when stocks "split"?**

When a stock price gets so high that investors are reluctant to buy, the company may declare a stock split. With a two-for-one split, you receive a free share of stock for every share you own, and the price per share is cut in half. The value of your investment doesn't change, but the lower price may make it more attractive to investors and demand for the stock may eventually push the price up. Since you have more shares, your investment is worth more than it would have been without the split. Stock splits don't always result in higher prices, though.

Question 217: **How do I buy stocks?**

You can buy stocks through a full-service brokerage or a discount brokerage by calling a stockbroker and placing an order, or you can use a discount Internet broker to execute your own orders. Make sure you understand all of the terms on the online form before finalizing your purchase. You don't need a full-service broker unless you want advice regarding which stocks you should buy. Brokers are paid on commission, so you should make up your own mind about what to buy or sell. The best way to invest is to do your research, choose a good stock or mutual fund, and stick with it for the long haul. There will no doubt be dips and rises, but historically the stock market has outperformed all other investments. You don't need to "churn" your stocks, buying and selling constantly and trying to anticipate ups and downs in the market. You can't afford to ignore changes in the financial condition of the companies you're invested in, but you shouldn't have to review their status more than quarterly.

Question 218: **What are bonds?**

Bonds are known as fixed-income securities because their income is fixed at the time the issuer sells them. When you buy a bond, you're lending the bond issuer money in return for a fixed rate of return. This interest is usually paid quarterly but is sometimes paid at the maturity date, when the issuer repays the principal it borrowed from you. Corporations, states, cities, and the federal government issue bonds for the same reason companies issue stock: to raise money for operations, expansion, or other financial needs.

Bonds issued by the federal government are extremely safe. Some corporate bonds are safe and others are high-risk. High-yield bonds pay a higher interest rate, but their nickname of "junk bonds" should give you fair warning of their risk. One of the risks associated with bonds is related to interest rates. If you lock in your money for a number of years at a fixed interest rate, you could be stuck if market rates go up. You may not be able to sell the bond for full price if other bonds are paying higher interest rates.

Question 219: **How can I buy government bonds?**

You can buy federal government bonds, including U.S. savings bonds, directly from the U.S. Treasury, and both government and corporate bonds through a stockbroker. If you don't want to buy individual bonds, you can buy shares in a bond fund, which invests in a number of different bonds. You'll incur fund expenses that will eat at your return, so bond funds are best if you'd rather pay a fee for broad diversification and professional management instead of choosing the bonds yourself.

Question 220: **Why should I consider going with index funds?**

If you don't want to spend a lot of time keeping up with the financial status of the companies you're invested in, and you don't want to pay a manager to pick stocks, a stock index mutual fund is the best choice. The largest and best-known stock index fund is Vanguard's S&P 500 fund. Over the last decade it has outperformed 90 percent of all other mutual funds, while having one of the lowest expense ratios in the market.

Question 221: **What are mutual funds?**

Mutual funds are a way for investors to pool their money so they can invest in many different stocks. Each investor is charged a percentage of his or her investment as a fee to pay the expenses of having a professional fund manager and all the costs associated with researching, buying, and selling stocks. Like stocks, some mutual funds are riskier than others, so be sure to read the fund's objectives and know what it invests in. Will your money be buying stocks in blue-chip companies or in the corporations of developing countries? Although past performance is no guarantee of the future, look at how the fund has done over the last several years and compare it to an applicable index to see if it kept pace with its competitors. Also consider the expense ratio. The lower it is, the more of your return you get to pocket.

Question 222: Where can I go to purchase mutual funds?

You can use full-service or discount brokers to buy mutual funds, or you can buy directly from a family of mutual funds, like Vanguard *(www.vanguard.com)* or Fidelity *(www.fidelity.com)*. Call the company's toll-free number or request an investor's kit online, fill out the forms, and send them in with your check. You can initiate this procedure on the mutual fund's website, but you'll still have to send in your check—unless you want to transfer the money electronically.

Question 223: What is the difference between load and no-load funds?

Load is a sales fee or commission charged by some mutual funds, and is usually stated as a percentage of the amount purchased or sold. Front-end loads are fees charged upfront when you buy the fund. Back-end loads are fees you pay when you sell the fund. If the load is 6 percent and you invest $2,000, the load will be $120. Funds that don't charge front-end or back-end loads are called no-load funds. When choosing a mutual fund, consider the load, if any, and the annual expense ratio. These eat into your return. If you buy a fund with a 6 percent load and a 2 percent expense ratio, you have to earn an 8 percent return the first year before you break even.

Question 224: Should I hire a financial planner?

Using expert advice is not a guarantee that your investments will make money. If you have the time and interest to do your own research and educate yourself, you probably don't need a financial planner for choosing investments, unless you have a complex situation. Consider developing your own written financial plans, but meet every few years with a financial planner to make sure there are no glaring issues or gaps in the course you've charted for yourself.

Don't ever rely totally on another person to make investment decisions for you. If you use a professional, educate yourself about the recommended investments and be involved in the buying and selling decisions he or she executes on your behalf. Many financial planners earn commissions from the companies they deal with, so they may not be entirely objective when making recommendations. You can avoid this problem by choosing a fee-only planner who is paid by the hour and doesn't benefit from recommending one investment over another.

Chapter 17

PREPARING FOR RETIREMENT

YOU'RE NEVER TOO young to start investing for retirement. Compounding of earnings is so powerful that if you start investing in your twenties, you can amass a large nest egg with little effort by the time you are in your sixties or seventies. All that's required is a basic understanding of retirement plans and the commitment to start now.

If you're in your twenties or thirties, you may feel like you have all the time in the world to invest for retirement. Don't find out the hard way that you can't start in your forties and expect to catch up to those who started in their twenties. The younger you are when you start, the less you'll need to invest, thanks to the power of compounding and the length of time until retirement.

It's difficult to think ahead to your retirement when you're young. There are so many things you want to do and so little money at your disposal. Yet investing a relatively small amount of money in your twenties can save you from having to invest much more when you're in your forties and fifties in order to be able to live comfortably in retirement.

Question 225: **What is a defined-contribution plan?**

With defined-contribution plans, you're in the driver's seat when it comes to deciding how your money will be invested. You'll choose from a variety of stock or bond mutual funds, guaranteed funds, annuities, cash equivalents like money market accounts, or your company's stock. The following are the most common defined-contribution plans:

- 401(k) plans, offered by private companies
- 403(b) plans, offered by nonprofit, tax-exempt employers, such as schools and colleges, hospitals, museums, and foundations
- 457 plans, offered by federal, state, and local government agencies and nonprofit organizations

Other defined-contribution plans include ESOPs, money purchase plans, profit-sharing plans, simplified employee pension (SEP) plans, savings incentive match plans (SIMPLEs), and thrift or savings plans (TSAs). These plans all have one important thing in common: You pay no taxes on your contributions or your earnings until you withdraw the money.

Question 226: **How can I save money through my 401(k) plan?**

The 401(k) plan gives a special tax break to employees saving for retirement. If you contribute $2,000 a year and you're in the 28 percent federal tax bracket, you'll save $560 because the $2,000 is deducted from your pay before your taxes are calculated. If you live in one of the states where 401(k) contributions are tax-deferred, and you're in a 6 percent state income tax bracket, you'll save another $120 in state taxes, for a total savings of $680.

The bottom line is that you add $2,000 to your investment account but only $1,320 comes out of your pocket ($2,000 – $680 = $1,320). It's like getting a raise. You don't pay taxes on your earnings until you withdraw them, presumably at retirement, so your investments grow faster as your untaxed earnings benefit from compounding.

Question 227: **Why are there limits to how much I can contribute to my 401(k)?**

The IRS sets limits, adjusted annually for inflation, on how much you can contribute to a 401(k) plan each year. For 2002, you can contribute up to $11,000 as long as it doesn't exceed 25 percent of your combined wages and your employer's contributions.

Your employer is subject to strict IRS regulations to ensure that your 401(k) plan doesn't discriminate against lower-paid employees. If you're a highly compensated employee, your contributions will be limited by how much the less highly compensated employees contribute. Highly compensated employees are defined as those who made $90,000 or more in the prior year or owned 5 percent or more of the company.

Question 228: **What is "vesting"?**

You're always 100 percent vested in your own contributions to the plan. The employer match is often subject to vesting, which means you earn the right to it gradually, over a number of years of employment with the company. There are two types of vesting schedules. About half of all 401(k) plans have cliff vesting, where you don't own any of the matching contributions until you've worked for the company for a certain amount of time. The Tax Relief Act of 2001 shortened the maximum vesting schedule for cliff vesting to no more than three years. The other type of vesting schedule is graded vesting, where you own an increasing percentage of the employer match over several years. Under the Tax Relief Act of 2001, vesting must take place in no more than 6 years. A typical vesting schedule will now be 20 percent after the second year, 40 percent after the third year, 60 percent after the fourth year, 80 percent after the fifth year, and 100 percent after the sixth year.

Question 229: **What happens to my 401(k) if I find a new job?**

The portability of 401(k) plans is a great feature, but what do you do with your money when you change jobs? You have three choices:

1. If you have over $5,000 in your account, you may leave your funds in your employer's plan.
2. You may be able to roll your balance over into your new employer's plan.
3. You can set up an individual retirement account (IRA) at a bank, through a broker, or directly with a mutual fund.

If your plan has cliff vesting, and you leave before working the required number of years, you walk away from everything your employer has contributed as matching funds, which could be a substantial amount. You could possibly earn thousands of additional dollars in company matching funds by staying in your current job for a few more months or years.

Question 230: **How is a 403(b) plan different from a 401(k)?**

403(b) plans are defined-contribution plans used by nonprofit organizations. They work very much like 401(k) plans. Your contributions are tax-deductible and your earnings are tax-deferred until you take the money out at retirement. Like 401(k) plans, the amounts that you and your employer can contribute are limited by law.

Question 231: **What is an IRA?**

Individual retirement accounts or IRAs have evolved in the more than twenty years since they were established and now include such variations as SEP IRAs, Roth IRAs, SIMPLE IRAs, and more. IRAs provide the same tax-deferred benefits as 401(k) and similar employer-sponsored plans and allow you to decide how your funds will be invested.

If you have employment income, you could contribute up to 10 percent of your income each year, not to exceed $3,000 in 2002, to an IRA. The limit was set to increase to $4,000 in 2005 and now it's $5,000 in 2008. You can set up an IRA through most banks and financial institutions, or through a mutual fund company or broker. You can start making withdrawals at age fifty-nine and a half, and you must start doing so by age seventy and a half. Like 401(k) plans, a 10 percent penalty is placed on any funds you take out early unless you retire, need the money to pay medical expenses, or are disabled.

Question 232: **Do I need to open an IRA?**

Contributing to an IRA doesn't make sense unless you're maximizing your contributions to your 401(k) or 403(b) plan by contributing the IRS limit. Take full advantage of these employer-sponsored defined-contribution plans first and if you have money left to invest for retirement, consider IRAs. If you don't have access to an employer-sponsored plan, then by all means, invest as much as possible in IRAs.

Use the online calculators at Leadfusion, Inc. (*www .leadfusion.com*) to help you determine which IRA you're eligible for and whether you should convert your IRA to a Roth IRA. The site also offers other IRA-related tools.

Question 233: **How should I invest my retirement funds?**

With retirement investing, it's important to think long-term. Because retirement earnings grow tax-deferred and you have many years before you'll make withdrawals, retirement plans are best suited for your most aggressive investing, which means stocks and mutual funds. Don't make the mistake of putting all your money in money market funds or guaranteed investment contracts (GICs). Diversify your portfolio to balance risk and reward and you should come out far ahead in the long term. This doesn't mean you shouldn't choose your investments carefully. If 80 percent of your retirement funds are in stock mutual funds, most of it should be in well-established funds with a history of solid performance. If you want to get aggressive with some of your money, you can place a small percentage of your stock investments in higher-risk funds.

Question 234: **What are annuities?**

When you buy an annuity, you sign a contract with an insurance company that stipulates the amount of your investment, whether you choose a fixed or variable rate for interest, the method of payment, and any fees. Fixed-rate annuities guarantee a specific interest rate for the life of the annuity. Interest rates on variable-rate annuities fluctuate with the ups and downs of the financial markets. You can invest with one lump-sum payment or build it gradually over time.

Question 235: **Should I buy an annuity?**

Your earnings grow tax-deferred, but the money you put in is not tax-deductible, so this is an investment best suited for someone who has taken full advantage of all the tax-deductible plans available and still has money left over to invest. It's unlikely that the average person in her or his twenties or thirties would choose this investment vehicle, but you should be aware of it in case an insurance agent attempts to sell you one.

Question 236: **Can I count on receiving Social Security benefits when I retire?**

By 2037 the taxes collected will pay only 72 percent of benefits owed. While there's no reason to fear that the system will be bankrupt, it's clear that you shouldn't rely on Social Security for more than half of your retirement income. There was a time when many retirees relied on Social Security to get them through their golden years. Today Social Security is considered a supplement to your retirement income, not the main source.

Question 237: **How can I find out how much I might receive from Social Security?**

When you reach retirement age, you'll receive benefits based on a complex calculation using the number of years you worked, the income you earned during those years, and your age at retirement. You can compute estimates of your future Social Security benefits and get information about the factors that influence your benefit amount by visiting the planner and calculator section of the Social Security Administration's website at *www.ssa.gov.*

There's been much discussion about whether Social Security is going broke. It appears that the system will be able to meet all benefit payment requirements for the next thirty years, but that may not be the case when you retire. Sixty-five million baby boomers will put a strain on the system when they start collecting benefits, but some experts project that even then they'll be able to pay 75 percent of the benefits that workers have earned. This will probably equate to no more than 40 percent of your preretirement income and will fall far short of what you'll need for even the simplest lifestyle.

Chapter 18

CREATING AN ESTATE PLAN

IN YOUR TWENTIES and thirties estate planning may seem like a low priority, but don't fall under the misconception that it's only for the elderly or the wealthy. Tragedy can strike at any age. Planning for the unexpected is best done today, especially if you have a family.

Some aspects of estate planning are important only if you have a very large estate or are elderly. Those issues won't be covered here. Instead, we'll discuss the issues that may apply to you in your twenties and thirties. For most people, writing a will is a very simple and inexpensive procedure, yet over 70 percent of Americans die intestate. Addressing issues of guardianship for your children and disposition of your assets in a will is the only way to ensure that these things are handled as you wish.

Question 238: **I feel like I'm too young for estate planning. Do I really need to be thinking about these things now?**

If you own anything or have kids, for example, you need a will. A durable power of health care and durable power of attorney are important to ensure that your wishes are carried out if you become incapacitated by accident or illness and are unable to make your own health care and financial decisions. Regardless of how simple your estate plan is at this point in your life, review it whenever significant events take place. If you marry, divorce, remarry, or have a child, you may want to make changes to your will. If you move to another state, make sure your will complies with the laws in that state and is still valid. If the value of your assets changes significantly, you may want to review the terms of your will and decide if any changes are in order. If one of your heirs dies, you should change your will to remove that person. If the executor of your will, administrator of your trust, or the guardian you appointed for your kids dies or becomes incapacitated, make changes immediately.

Question 239: **When do I need to write a will?**

As soon as you acquire your first assets as an adult (car, stocks, bonds, stereo equipment, savings accounts), get married, or have a baby, you should make a will. If you die intestate (without a will) the state will determine who gets what. More importantly, the state will decide who will gain guardianship over your minor children, regardless of what your wishes were and who you expressed them to. Don't operate under the common misconception that if you die intestate, your spouse will inherit all your property. In fact, if you have kids, in most states your spouse will receive between one-third and one-half of your assets and the rest will be split among your kids, no matter how young they are.

Question 240: **I'm married, so if I died my spouse would inherit all my assets, right?**

If you're married with no kids, in most states your spouse will get one-third of your assets and your parents will get the rest. If your parents aren't alive, your siblings will inherit. In some states, your children from a previous marriage or relationship could be disinherited and your entire estate could go to your new spouse. If you're unmarried and childless, the state will divide your estate among your relatives as it sees fit.

If you're in your twenties, single, and don't own much, you may feel that a will is unnecessary. Still, you probably own things that don't have any great monetary value but do have sentimental value and that you'd like a particular person to have. There may be other things you'd rather didn't end up in someone else's hands.

Question 241: **What should I include in my will?**

The first step in estate planning is getting a handle on what you own so you can decide whom to leave it to. If you've followed the advice in Chapter 1, you've already prepared a net worth statement and have a good grasp on the value of your assets and belongings. To this list, add those items that have meaning to you but may not have a significant monetary value, like family photo albums, personal journals, book or record collections, and pets.

Decide how you want your assets distributed if you die. For your primary beneficiaries, use percentages, not fixed dollar amounts, so that your will remains up-to-date as your assets increase or decrease. You can use fixed dollar amounts for secondary beneficiaries, for instance, if you want to leave money to a niece or nephew that you dote on.

Question 242: **Do I need to hire an attorney to draw up my will?**

Unless your estate is very large or you have complex issues to cover, you can draw up your own legal will without paying for an attorney. There are good books available to guide you through the process, but the best way to do it yourself is by using computer software like Quicken Lawyer Personal, which walks you through the process by asking questions, and then generates a will that is legal in all fifty states.

Question 243: **How can I make sure my will is a legal document?**

For a will to become legal, it should be typed or computer-generated. Handwritten wills are legally binding in only twenty-five states and those states have different requirements about signing the pages and other issues, so it's much safer to have it typewritten. Your will must state that it's your will and it must be signed and dated; at least two (in some states three) people who won't inherit anything under the will must witness your signature and sign their names to the will. The witnesses must watch you sign and you must watch them sign. They don't need to read the will or know what's in it.

Question 244: **Should I put instructions for my funeral arrangements in my will?**

Your will isn't a good place to state your wishes about your final arrangements because it may not be located and read until long after it's too late to follow your wishes. If you don't leave written instructions, the right to make these decisions will most likely rest with those closest to you, in this order: spouse, child or children, parent or parents, the next of kin, or a public administrator appointed by a court. You can prevent disagreements by putting your wishes in writing. Your instructions may include the following:

- Whether you want to be embalmed.
- Whether you want to be cremated or buried.
- Your preference for the mortuary that will handle your burial or cremation.
- The type of casket or other container your remains will be placed in for burial or cremation.
- Your wishes regarding the funeral.
- Who your pallbearers will be.
- Where you want your remains to be scattered.
- What kind of marker you want where your remains are buried.

Question 245: **How can I become an organ donor?**

Successful tissue and organ transplants have created a great demand for organ donations. If you wish to donate your organs, you should obtain an organ donor card from a local hospital or your state's Department of Motor Vehicles. Most states have a method of indicating on your driver's license that you're an organ donor. Discussing your wishes with family and friends will help increase the likelihood that your organs will actually be used.

Question 246: **What is included in a living will?**

Most people have strong feelings about the type of health care they would or wouldn't want to receive if they were unable to make health care decisions for themselves. An advance medical directive, popularly known as a living will, is a document you create while you're healthy that specifies how you want to be treated if you're terminally ill or incapacitated. By making your wishes known ahead of time, you'll receive the care you want and save your loved ones some of the anguish of making difficult decisions on your behalf. Your living will can cover issues such as organ donation, funeral arrangements, and hospital or nursing home arrangements, as well as acceptable medical treatments.

Question 247: **How should I choose a health care proxy?**

A health care proxy is the person you designate to make sure the health care decisions you included in your living will are carried out if you're incapacitated or unable to communicate on your own behalf. Usually, a health care proxy is a family member or close friend. Regardless of who it is, you should discuss your wishes with him or her in detail.

You should also discuss this with your primary care physician and make sure your physician has a copy in your file. Other copies should go to the person you designate as your health care proxy and your attorney, and a copy should be kept in your personal files. You must sign the document in the presence of two adult witnesses who are not the person you've appointed as your proxy.

Question 248: **What is a durable power of attorney?**

A durable power of attorney (a form that must be signed in front of a notary public) allows you to appoint a trusted agent to manage your financial affairs if you become unable to do so yourself due to physical disability or mental incapacity. The power of attorney lasts until your death, unless you revoke it. The person you give power of attorney to can enter into contracts, negotiate, pay bills, buy and sell property, and handle your other financial affairs on your behalf if you're not able to.

These documents are important for elderly people who may suffer from Alzheimer's disease or senile dementia, but they have to be created and signed while the person still has their mental faculties. You may become acquainted with durable power of attorney long before you need one yourself because your parents or an older relative may ask you to become their durable power of attorney.

Question 249: **How can I set up a trust?**

A trust is a legal arrangement allowing for the transfer of property to a trustee who holds it for the benefit of another person, the beneficiary. You can be the trustee of your own trust and maintain total control, or you can indicate one or more trustees to administer your trust.

After you set up a trust, you have to fund it by transferring property from your name to the trust. There are legal fees associated with setting up a trust and your situation may not warrant the expense. If you do decide to set one up, find a reputable lawyer who specializes in estate planning; don't buy a do-it-yourself kit or fall for high-pressure sales techniques from companies pushing trusts.

Question 250: **How can I minimize estate taxes?**

Your estate consists of everything you own, from real estate to jewelry, stocks and bonds, life insurance policies, bank accounts, a business, 401(k) funds, and other items of value. When you die, everything you leave to your surviving spouse is transferred tax-free. You're allowed to transfer a certain amount to others tax-free during your lifetime as gifts and let your estate use the balance of the credit after your death.

The amount you can transfer without incurring a tax liability is determined by the Federal Unified Tax Credit, which in 2002 allows you to transfer $1,000,000 tax-free. While that seems like a very large amount, more and more people have estates of this size due to the increasing value of their homes, retirement funds, and life insurance policies. The federal taxes on the taxable amount of your estate can be as high as 55 percent. To reduce taxes and leave more to their heirs, many people set up trusts, which can be complex and expensive. In 2001, Congress passed a law that phases out estate taxes over a ten-year period, with total repeal taking place in 2010.

GLOSSARY OF FINANCIAL TERMS

PERSONAL FINANCE HAS a language all its own, but it doesn't have to be intimidating. The average person only needs to know the basics, so if you have an understanding of the terms in this glossary, you're off to a good start.

APR: Annual percentage rate; a way of expressing the interest rate on a loan. Because it includes fees that are paid upfront, it gives the borrower a more accurate picture of the true cost of borrowing.

asset: Anything you own that is of monetary value, including cash, stocks, bonds, mutual funds, cars, real estate, and other items.

bankruptcy: A court process in which you acknowledge that you are unable to pay your debts and you allow your assets to be sold to repay creditors to the extent possible (Chapter 7 or liquidation bankruptcy), or you work with the court to set up a plan to pay all or some of your debt over a period of several years (Chapter 13 or reorganization bankruptcy).

Blue Book value: The market value of a car after an allowance for depreciation is deducted. This is an estimate of what a seller can expect to receive for the vehicle upon resale, as posted in the *Kelley Blue Book*.

bonds: Loans from investors to corporations and governments given in exchange for interest payments and timely repayment of the debt. Interest rates are usually fixed.

budget: A forecast of income and expenses by category. Actual expenses and income are compared to the forecast and a plan is developed to reduce or control expenses to provide for savings to meet financial goals.

CD: Certificate of deposit; money lent to banks for a set period of time, usually between one month and five years, in exchange for compound interest, usually at a fixed rate.

COBRA: Consolidated Omnibus Reconciliation Act; a federal law that requires most employers to allow terminating employees to continue their health insurance coverage at the employee's expense, for a limited time.

compound interest: If interest earned on an investment is calculated only on the original amount invested, it's known as simple interest. If interest earned is calculated on the original amount plus any previously earned interest, it's known as compound interest, which makes the investment grow more quickly.

defined-contribution retirement plan: A retirement plan offered by employers that allows employees to contribute to the plan but does not guarantee a predetermined benefit at retirement. 401(k), 403(b), 457, and profit-sharing plans are examples.

DRIP: Dividend reinvestment plans allow investors to automatically reinvest their dividends in the company's stock rather than receive them in cash. Many companies waive the sales charges for stock purchased under the DRIP.

escrow: Money or other assets held by an agent until the terms of a contract or agreement are fulfilled. Many mortgage companies require borrowers to pay prorated property taxes monthly with their mortgage payment. These funds are held in an escrow account until payment is due to the local government.

foreclosure: A legal process that terminates an owner's right to a property, usually because the borrower defaults on payments. Home foreclosures usually result in a forced sale of the property to pay off the mortgage.

head of household: A tax-filing status that provides tax breaks to single parents who maintain a home for one or more eligible dependents.

intestate: Dying without a will that specifies who should receive the property and personal belongings of the deceased.

IRA: Individual retirement account; a retirement account that anyone who has earned income can contribute to. Amounts contributed to traditional IRAs are usually tax-deferred. Amounts contributed to Roth IRAs are not deductible but taxes are never due on the earnings.

joint tenancy with right of survivorship: Shared ownership of property by two or more people, giving the surviving owner(s) rights to a deceased owner's share. See also tenancy in common.

liability: An amount owed to creditors or others. Common liabilities include mortgage, car payments, student loans, and credit card debt.

lien: A legal claim against an asset, usually used to secure a loan.

living will: A legal document used to specify what, if any, life-prolonging measures a person wants if he or she becomes terminally ill or incapacitated.

load: A sales charge or commission paid to a broker or other third-party when mutual funds are bought or sold. Front-end loads are sometimes incurred when an investor purchases the shares and back-end loads are sometimes incurred when investors sell the shares.

marriage tax penalty: A feature of the U.S. tax system that results in married couples paying more in taxes than they would if they were single.

mutual fund: An investment that allows thousands of investors to pool their money to purchase stocks, bonds, or other types of investments, depending on the objectives of the fund.

net worth: The value of all of a person's assets (anything owned that has a monetary value) minus all of the person's liabilities (amounts owed to others).

nonmarital agreement: A written agreement between two unmarried people living together, spelling out how their finances will be handled.

PMI: Private mortgage insurance; insurance that protects a lender if a borrower defaults on a mortgage. Lenders require PMI if the mortgage exceeds 80 percent of the appraised value of the home.

points: Finance charges paid by a borrower when a loan is initiated. One point is worth 1 percent of the loan amount. Borrowers can "buy down" an interest rate to get a lower rate by paying points upfront.

probate: A court process to determine the validity of a will and oversee the distribution of property upon the owner's death.

risk tolerance: An investor's ability to tolerate fluctuations in the value of an investment in the expectation of receiving a higher return.

rollover: Reinvestment of a distribution from a qualified retirement plan into an IRA or another qualified plan in order to retain its tax-deferred status and avoid taxes and penalties for early withdrawal.

Rule of 72: A method of estimating the time it will take for a certain amount of money to double at a given interest rate (72 divided by the interest rate equals roughly the number of years it will take for the money to double).

standard deduction: The fixed amount deducted from adjusted gross income allowed taxpayers who don't itemize deductions.

stock: An ownership share in a corporation, entitling the investor to a pro rata share of the corporation's earnings and assets.

tenancy in common: Shared ownership of property by two or more people, giving each owner the legal right to pass on his or her share of the property to any other person in a written will. See also joint tenancy with right of survivorship.

term life insurance: Life insurance that pays the beneficiary a predetermined amount of money as long as the covered individual dies within a specified period of time (the term of the policy).

whole life insurance: Life insurance that covers an individual for his or her whole life rather than a specified term. Whole life policies contain a savings component that allows cash to accumulate over time.

will: A legal document that specifies how a person's belongings will be disposed of upon his or her death. It can also identify a legal guardian for children.

401(k): A defined-contribution retirement plan that allows participants to contribute pretax dollars to various investments.

INTERNET RESOURCES

IN THIS DAY and age, one of the greatest resources available to us is the world wide web. There are an astounding number of websites out there. Some are very helpful, but others may have a hidden agenda or be a scam. The websites listed in this appendix are reputable sources of information. Although many of them offer paid services, there are plenty of useful insights that you can get for free.

Banking

Bankrate.com, *www.bankrate.com*
StopATMFees.com, *www.stopatmfees.com*
Federal Trade Commission, *www.ftc.gov*
Federal Deposit Insurance Corporation, *www.fdic.gov*

Budgeting and Saving Money

Financial Planning at About.com, *http://financialplan.about.com*
Personal Budgeting and Money Saving Tips, *www.personal-budget-planning-saving-money.com*
The Dollar Stretcher, *www.stretcher.com*
Frugal Living at About.com, *www.frugalliving.about.com*

Cars

Autos at MSN, *http://www.autos.msm.com*
Autobytel, *www.autobytel.com*
CarBuyingTips.com, *www.carbuyingtips.com*
CarInfo.com, *www.carinfo.com*
Consumer Reports, *www.consumerreports.org*
Edmunds, *www.edmunds.com*
IntelliChoice, *www.intellichoice.com*
Kelley Blue Book, *www.kbb.com*
AutoTrader.com, *www.autotrader.com*
LeaseGuide.com, *www.leaseguide.com*
Warranty Direct, *www.warrantydirect.com*
1SourceAutoWarranty.com, *www.1sourceautowarranty.com*

Consumer Information

Consumer World, *www.consumerworld.org*
ConsumerREVIEW, *www.consumerreview.com*
Better Business Bureau, *www.bosbbb.org*

Credit and Debt

National Foundation for Credit Counseling, *www.nfcc.org*
Consumer Credit Counseling Service, *www.cccsintl.org*

Bankrate.com, *www.bankrate.com*
Myvesta, *www.getoutofdebt.org*

Credit-Reporting Bureaus

Equifax, *www.equifax.com*
Experian, *www.experian.com*
TransUnion, *www.transunion.com*

Employee Ownership

National Center for Employee Ownership, *www.nceo.org*

Financial Advice

The Motley Fool, *www.fool.com*
CNNMoney, *http://money.cnn.com*
Financial Planning at About.com, *http://financialplan.about.com*
AskMen.com, *www.askmen.com*
MSN Money, *http://moneycentral.msn.com*
Quicken, *www.quicken.com*
MsMoney.com, *www.msmoney.com*
SmartMoney.com, *www.smartmoney.com*
NewlywedFinances.com, *www.newlywedfinances.com*

Financial Calculators

FinanCenter.com, *www.financenter.com*
Java Financial Calculators, *www.dinkytown.net*
Financial Calculators, *www.fincalc.com*

Fraud

The National Fraud Information Center, *www.fraud.org*
The Federal Trade Commission, *www.ftc.gov*
National Association of Attorneys General, *www.naag.org*
Contractor Fraud, *www.contractorfraud.net*

Home Buying

National Association of Realtors, *www.realtor.com*
Homestore.com, *www.homestore.com*

Insurance

Northwestern Mutual Financial Network, *www.lifeinsurance.com*
Insure.com, *www.insure.com*
Insurance Information Institute, *www.iii.org*
Health Insurance Association of America, *www.hiaa.org*

Investing

Morningstar.com, *www.morningstar.com*
Investing Online Resource Center, *www.investingonline.org*
Savings Bonds from the Treasury Department, *www.savingsbond.gov*

Job/Occupational Information

U.S. Bureau of Labor Statistics, *www.bls.gov*
Monster.com, *www.monster.com*
Job Search at About.com, *http://jobsearch.about.com*

Legal Advice

Nolo, *www.nolo.com*

Loans and Mortgages

Fair Credit Reporting Act, *www.ftc.gov/os/statutes/fcrajump.shtm*
Mortgage Expo.com, *www.mortgageexpo.com*
E-Loan, *www.eloan.com*
HSH Associates, *www.hsh.com*
Mortgage101.com, *www.mortgage101.com*

Money and Young People

Kids' Money, *www.kidsmoney.org*
Young Money, *www.youngmoney.com*

Moving

National Association of Realtors, *www.homefair.com*
Fannie Mae, *www.fanniemae.com*
Moving Center, *www.movingcenter.com*

Renting

Rentlaw.com, *www.rentlaw.com*
ApartmentGuide.com, *www.apartmentguide.com*

Retirement

RetirementPlanner.org, *www.retirementplanner.org*
Social Security Administration, *www.ssa.gov*
American Association of Retired Persons, *www.aarp.org*
Profit Sharing Council of America, *www.401k.org*
Roth IRA, *www.rothira.com*

Student Loans

Northwest Education Loan Association, *www.nela.net*
Sallie Mae, *www.salliemae.com*

Taxes

H&R Block, *www.hrblock.com*
WorldWideWeb Tax, *www.wwwebtax.com*
Internal Revenue Service (IRS), *www.irs.gov*
TurboTax software, *www.turbotax.com*
National Association of Tax Professionals, *www.taxprofessionals.com*

LIST OF QUESTIONS

Part I: Getting Started

Chapter 1: Setting Goals

Question 1: Why do I need to set financial goals?

Question 2: What should I do first?

Question 3: Why do I need a net worth statement?

Question 4: How do I create my net worth statement?

Question 5: Should I include my life insurance policy in my net worth statement?

Question 6: Where can I find out what my car is worth?

Question 7: What do I do after I list all my assets?

Question 8: Now that I've listed my assets and liabilities, how do I calculate my net worth?

Question 9: If I have a negative net worth, should I use my savings to pay off some of my debts?

Question 10: What should my financial goals be?

Question 11: I have a long list of goals—which ones should I start working toward first?

Question 12: How will I know if I'm making any progress?

Question 13: What should I do if I fall behind on achieving my goals?

Question 14: Where can I find good information on personal finance?

Question 15: Can I find trustworthy information on the Internet?

Chapter 2: Building a Budget

Question 16: Why do I need to create a budget?

Question 17: What are the benefits of budgeting?

Question 18: What goes into making a good budget?

Question 19: What should I include in my budget?

Question 20: How can I save money when my budget shows me that I spend all my income?

Question 21: How do I figure out where all my money is going?

Question 22: Do I have to keep track of all the little things, like my daily cup of coffee?

Question 23: How can I use my budget to save money?

Question 24: How much should I be spending in each category?

Question 25: How do I know if I'll have enough money at the end of the month?

Question 26: What should I do if I can't stick to a monthly budget?

Question 27: How can I cut back on essentials, like groceries?

Question 28: Do I need to use a software program to manage my money?

Question 29: What can I do to stay motivated and keep to my budget?

Chapter 3: Saving Money

Question 30: Why should I worry about saving money now?

Question 31: What is compound interest?

Question 32: How is compound interest calculated?

Question 33: What is the Rule of 72?

Question 34: How does the Rule of 72 work?

Question 35: In what other ways can I use the Rule of 72?

Question 36: What is inflation?

Question 37: How does inflation affect me?

Question 38: What does "the time value of money" mean?

Question 39: Do I really need an emergency fund?

Question 40: I can barely cover my living expenses each month—how can I save anything?

Question 41: If I can only save a few dollars each month, should I even bother?

Question 42: What should I do to start saving?

Question 43: What if there is no room in my budget for saving?

Chapter 4: Banking with Confidence

Question 44: How do I choose the right bank for me?

Question 45: Should I consider using a credit union?

Question 46: How do I know my money will be safe?

Question 47: What are opportunity costs?

Question 48: How can I reduce the costs of banking?

Question 49: Should I keep all my money in my checking account?

Question 50: What is overdraft protection?

Question 51: How can I avoid overdraft fees?

Question 52: What should I do to minimize ATM fees?

Question 53: What can I do to prevent identity theft?

Question 54: If someone steals my debit card, will I be responsible for the thief's charges?

Question 55: What's the best way to confirm that the bank has not made any errors on my accounts?

Question 56: Aside from a savings account, what is a better option for protecting and growing my savings?

Question 57: What is a CD?

Question 58: Should I put my money into a CD?

Part II: Managing Debt

Chapter 5: Tackling Student Loans

Question 59: Once I'm out of school, when do I have to start repaying my loans?

Question 60: How can I qualify for a deferment?

Question 61: What options do I have if I can't get a deferment?

Question 62: What can I do to qualify for a forbearance?

Question 63: When deciding on a repayment plan, should I just choose the one with the lowest monthly payment?

Question 64: Is it to possible to have my loans forgiven altogether?

Question 65: What is a Stafford loan?

Question 66: How is a federal Perkins loan different from other loans?

Question 67: Can I defer my Perkins loan?

Question 68: Is there any reason why I shouldn't take a deferment or forbearance if I qualify for one?

Question 69: What if I can't make the payments on my student loan?

Question 70: What does it mean to be "in default" of a loan?

Question 71: How would defaulting on my student loan affect me?

Question 72: What can I do to minimize the damage after I've defaulted on my loan?

Question 73: Should I consolidate my student loans?

Chapter 6: Handling Credit Cards

Question 74: What's the definition of a credit card?

Question 75: What are some of the costs of having credit cards?

Question 76: What should I look for when choosing a credit card?

Question 77: Should I choose a card that gives me frequent flier miles or cash back on my purchases?

Question 78: What kind of interest rate should I be paying?

Question 79: Can I get a credit card even if I have damaged credit?

Question 80: What should I consider when applying for credit cards?

Question 81: What is a secured credit card?

Question 82: Should I take advantage of the cash advances my credit card company offers me?

Question 83: What is a credit report?

Question 84: Why do I need to know what's on my credit report?

Question 85: Why should I make more than the minimum monthly payment every month?

Question 86: If I have too much credit card debt, how can I start to pay it off?

Question 87: What should I do once I've paid off my credit card with the highest interest rate?

Question 88: Should I use a credit counseling service to help pay off my debts?

Question 89: Should I buy a new or a used car?

Question 90: I've found a used car I really like—what do I do next?

Question 91: Should I trade my old car in to the dealership?

Question 92: What are my payment options when I want to buy a new or used car?

Question 93: How is a lease different from a loan?

Question 94: When should I consider leasing instead of buying?

Question 95: What are the disadvantages of leasing?

Question 96: How can I save money when buying a new car?

Question 97: How do I negotiate the price with the car dealer?

Question 98: Aside from the initial price, what else should I consider when buying a new car?

Question 99: How do I know how much I will be paying in insurance?

Question 100: Should I take the dealer's offer of an extended warranty?

Question 101: What is Chapter 13 bankruptcy?

Question 102: After I file for Chapter 13 bankruptcy, how much of my debts will I have to pay?

Question 103: What debts will I still be responsible for after filing for bankruptcy?

Question 104: How do I know if I'm eligible to file for Chapter 13 bankruptcy?

Question 105: How does Chapter 7 bankruptcy differ from Chapter 13 bankruptcy?

Question 106: What happens after I sign the Reaffirmation Statement?

Question 107: How do I know if I should file for Chapter 7 bankruptcy?

Question 108: What debts will I have to repay under Chapter 7?

Question 109: If I've incurred large debts that I cannot pay, can filing for bankruptcy help turn my life around?

Question 110: How can I avoid having to file for bankruptcy?

Question 111: What should I do before I file for bankruptcy?

Question 112: If I want to avoid bankruptcy, can a credit repair clinic help?

Part III: Getting Established

Chapter 9: Launching Your Career

Question 113: Where can I learn more about a company I am interested in working for?

Question 114: How should I go about evaluating the job itself?

Question 115: When I get a job offer, how will I know if the salary is reasonable?

Question 116: How can I make sure I'm getting the right salary and benefits package?

Question 117: When should I bring up the question of salary with my prospective employer?

Question 118: My new employer offers a flexible spending account to all employees. What is it and how does it work?

Question 119: I don't expect to retire for another thirty years or more. Should I start to contribute to my employer's retirement plan now?

Question 120: What are stock options?

Question 121: Should I participate in my company's employee stock ownership plan?

Question 122: What are incentive stock options?

Question 123: How do I ask my employer for a raise?

Question 124: How can I determine how much of a raise I should ask for?

Question 125: When should I ask for a raise?

Question 126: How do I know if I might be laid off?

Question 127: What should I do if I lose my job?

Chapter 10: Renting an Apartment

Question 128: How much can I afford to pay in rent?

Question 129: Should I consider moving back home?

Question 130: How can I find an apartment to rent?

Question 131: Should I use a Realtor to help me find an apartment?

Question 132: What should I consider when signing a lease?

Question 133: What if I need to leave before my lease ends?

Question 134: I don't want to commit to a one-year lease. Can I just rent on a month-to-month basis?

Question 135: How can I make sure I get my security deposit back when I leave?

Question 136: Will I have to pay to have my utilities (electricity, cable, etc.) turned on?

Question 137: Do I need to get renters' insurance?

Question 138: How much insurance coverage do I need?

Question 139: What's the difference between replacement cost and actual cash value?

Question 140: What is a deductible?

Question 141: How might moving to a new city affect what I pay for car insurance?

Chapter 11: Buying a Home

Question 142: What should I do before I start house hunting?

Question 143: Why do I need a down payment?

Question 144: How does a mortgage work?

Question 145: Do I need to get private mortgage insurance?

Question 146: How do mortgage terms differ?

Question 147: What is an adjustable-rate mortgage?

Question 148: Should I choose an ARM over a traditional mortgage?

Question 149: How does a balloon mortgage work?

Question 150: What are "points"?

Question 151: How can I determine the size of the mortgage I will need?

Question 152: What's the difference between being "preapproved" and being "prequalified" for a mortgage?

Question 153: How do I go about making an offer on the house I want?

Question 154: What happens after I've made an offer?

Question 155: The seller has accepted my offer. Now what?

Question 156: What are closing costs?

Chapter 12: Getting Married

Question 157: How can I start talking to my spouse about money matters?

Question 158: Should we share a joint account for all our income and paying all our bills?

Question 159: How should we divide the money-managing responsibilities?

Question 160: Do we need a prenuptial agreement?

Question 161: How can we save money on our wedding?

Question 162: What is the "marriage tax penalty"?

Question 163: How can we avoid a big tax bill in April?

Question 164: How can my new spouse and I start to combine our finances?

Question 165: What do I need to do if I'm changing my name?

Question 166: We are thinking about starting a family soon. How do we start planning for a new arrival?

Question 167: How do we handle our new family's health insurance needs?

Question 168: When should I start teaching my children about money?

Question 169: If my spouse and I get divorced, how can I protect myself financially?

Question 170: How can I protect my children in the event of a divorce?

Chapter 13: Staying Single

Question 171: Why do we need a nonmarital agreement?

Question 172: What's included in a nonmarital agreement?

Question 173: How is common-law marriage defined?

Question 174: If we're not planning to get married, why do we need to discuss our finances?

Question 175: What is a joint purchase agreement?

Question 176: How can we protect our rights if we want to buy a house together?

Question 177: How do we decide who gets the house if we break up?

Question 178: How should we divide household expenses if one of us earns significantly more than the other?

Question 179: Is it best to keep one joint or two separate bank accounts?

Question 180: If we own a house together, how do we decide who gets to take the mortgage deduction?

Question 181: Can one of us claim "head of household" status on our tax return even though we're not married?

Question 182: Why do I need a will?

Question 183: What is an advance directive?

PART IV: PLANNING FOR TOMORROW

Chapter 14: Insuring Your Future

Question 184: Do I need life insurance?

Question 185: How much does life insurance cost?

Question 186: I'm young and healthy—do I really need health insurance?

Question 187: What is an HMO?

Question 188: What's the difference between an HMO and a PPO?

Question 189: What is COBRA?

Question 190: How can I use my COBRA coverage?

Question 191: Why would I need disability insurance?

Question 192: What's the difference between short-term and long-term disability insurance?

Question 193: What is an "elimination period"?

Question 194: How is "disability" defined for insurance purposes?

Question 195: Why do I need homeowner's insurance?

Question 196: What types of homeowner's insurance are there?

Question 197: What is covered by auto insurance?

Chapter 15: Paying Taxes

Question 198: How do tax exemptions work?

Question 199: How can I determine my "effective tax rate"?

Question 200: What is the difference between itemized and standard deductions?

Question 201: I'm not an accountant—can I really file my taxes on my own?

Question 202: If I don't want to handle my taxes myself, how do I find someone I can trust to do it for me?

Question 203: What can I do to reduce my taxes?

Question 204: What types of records do I need to keep?

Question 205: How can I avoid being audited?

Question 206: How are returns chosen for audit?

Question 207: What should I do if I'm being audited?

Question 208: I owe money to the IRS this year, and I cannot afford to pay. What should I do?

Question 209: How can I make sure I don't owe money next year?

Chapter 16: Investing Wisely

Question 210: Where's the best place to invest my money?

Question 211: How do I know how much risk I can tolerate?

Question 212: What's the difference between high-risk and low-risk investments?

Question 213: What is asset allocation?

Question 214: How should I distribute my investments?

Question 215: Why do I need to diversify my assets?

Question 216: What does it mean when stocks "split"?

Question 217: How do I buy stocks?

Question 218: What are bonds?

Question 219: How can I buy government bonds?

Question 220: Why should I consider going with index funds?

Question 221: What are mutual funds?

Question 222: Where can I go to purchase mutual funds?

Question 223: What is the difference between load and no-load funds?

Question 224: Should I hire a financial planner?

Chapter 17: Preparing for Retirement

Question 225: What is a defined-contribution plan?

Question 226: How can I save money through my 401(k) plan?

Question 227: Why are there limits to how much I can contribute to my 401(k)?

Question 228: What is "vesting"?

Question 229: What happens to my 401(k) if I find a new job?

Question 230: How is a 403(b) plan different from a 401(k)?

Question 231: What is an IRA?

Question 232: Do I need to open an IRA?

Question 233: How should I invest my retirement funds?

Question 234: What are annuities?

Question 235: Should I buy an annuity?

Question 236: Can I count on receiving Social Security benefits when I retire?

Question 237: How can I find out how much I might receive from Social Security?

Chapter 18: Creating an Estate Plan

Question 238: I feel like I'm too young for estate planning. Do I really need to be thinking about these things now?

Question 239: When do I need to write a will?

Question 240: I'm married, so if I died my spouse would inherit all my assets, right?

Question 241: What should I include in my will?

Question 242: Do I need to hire an attorney to draw up my will?

Question 243: How can I make sure my will is a legal document?

Question 244: Should I put instructions for my funeral arrangements in my will?

Question 245: How can I become an organ donor?

Index